"It's hard to imagine a more pleasing journey through rural America than *Profoundly Country*—penned by farmer, ranch hand, cowboy, and open-hearted philosopher Dick Courteau. From the farms of Minnesota, to the rodeo rings of the mountain West, to the hardscrabble hills of Arkansas, here is a love song to America's open spaces—and to the lively, disarming, and often brilliant people whose lives unfold there. In these times of mass distraction, it's all too easy to lose touch with what it is in life that really matters. Not to worry. Wherever you are— big city or backwoods—this book will show you the way home…. The next time I'm asked that parlor question—what person would you really like to sit down and have a beer with—Dick will be on my short list!"

— Gary Ferguson, author, *The Eight Master Lessons of Nature*

"Dick Courteau grew up a student of rural America and the people living there. He's experienced several lifetimes in his 90 years: He's worked on a dairy farm and harvested sugar beets, traveled the rodeo circuit to be thrown from bulls and broncs, and packed his family of five in a covered wagon to flee an Arkansas drought behind a team of horses.

Reading *Profoundly Country*, you will experience first-hand the lives he led, learning essential truths about country life—the people he's met, the trials he's endured and the animals he's cared for and trained.

For of all the skills Dick has learned in his lifetime, I am most grateful for his aptitude to tell a story. His writing throbs with authenticity. Reading about any of the characters in these pages, you will come to know them better than if you met them on the street. Dick recalls details that take the reader to the exact location and time of the story. And his affinity for language makes taking that trip a delight."

— Joe Mischka, publisher, *Rural Heritage* magazine

"There's lots of folks writing about my home these days, or things that make me think about my home: country life, old-fashioned farming, and more. For my money, Dick Courteau's new collection gives us the best of it all. He may be from off, as we say, but when you make your way through these beautiful, thoughtful pieces, anybody can get a road map on how to do more than make do here in the hills. This is a gem of book—read it and savor it."

— Jared Phillips, author, *Hipbillies of the Ozarks*

"Come along readers and enjoy a walk through some reflections and recollections of Dick Courteau. His easy style of story-telling makes a person comfortable. It's as if you were enjoying a fireside chat around a bonfire in the dark of evening. Dick shares glimpses of his life in "the rurals" (farms, ranches and homesteads) from almost 90 years of memories. As a man who treasures reflections himself, I recommend this book with a smile and a country handshake."

— Ralph Rice, author, *Cultivating Memories*

Dick Courteau may call his collection tales of "Profoundly Country," but I would suggest that the reader may simply find them profoundly human, as well. We've seen over the years a search for something which is missing in the lives of many, and for many, that something has resulted in a return to their country roots; a life perhaps only heard of, but still much longed for. In *Profoundly Country,*" Mr. Courteau gives us a look at rural America between the end of the Second World War and the turn of the last century. I think many of those "searchers" who look to the country for that "thing missing in their lives" will find some good waypoints here—a little nostalgia, a lot of wisdom, with wit and honesty, entertaining to the last word.

—Jerry Hicks, author, *Tales From Carter Country*"

Profoundly Country

Memories and Meditations
of an Old Farmer/Cowboy

Profoundly Country

Memories and Meditations
of an Old Farmer/Cowboy

by Dick Courteau
with Jacqueline Courteau

Drawings by Maeve Courteau

*Photos by Daniel J. Kasztelan, Beverly Conley,
Caleb Courteau, and Don House*

Published by Mission Point Press
2554 Chandler Rd.
Traverse City, MI 49696
(231) 421-9513
MissionPointPress.com
ISBN: 978-1-961302-73-0
Library of Congress Control Number: 2024911174
Printed in the United States of America

Prior essays by Dick Courteau*

"The Good Life," *Rural Heritage*, August/September 2021, pp. 52–54

"Changing Times in the Boonies ," *Rural Heritage* August/September 2021, pp. 52–54.

"Profoundly Country" *Rural Heritage*, October/November 2023, pp. 26–31.

"Rural life hard but good: It takes perseverance and ingenuity" "Rural Life Hard But Good," *Rural Heritage* July/August 2023, pp. 24–25, and "Rural Ingenuity: Thinking Outside the box," *Rural Heritage* October/November 2023, pp. 80–81.

"How Ya Gonna Keep 'em Down on the Farm … When the Horses Get Under the Hood?" *Rural Heritage* December 2023/January 2024, pp. 10–12.

"My Western Welcome" *Rural Heritage* October/November 2021, pp. 30–33, (under the title "Cowboys and Indians").

"The Snake Beneath the Seat" *Rural Heritage* February/March 2022, pp. 56–61.

"Just Because You've Done it Before …" *Rural Heritage* February/March 2023, pp. 36–39.

"The Black Cow with the Red Eye" *Rural Heritage* December 2021/January 2022, pp. 28–29.

"Of Milk You Can't Drink, Horses That Can't Walk, and Crops Gone to Pot" *Rural Heritage* December 2021/January 2022, pp. 46–47.

"Out of the Mouths of Rubes" *Rural Heritage* June/July 2022, pp. 38–43.

"Country Justice Part 1: Country Justice from the Bench" *Rural Heritage* August/September 2022, pp. 22–24.

"Country Justice Part 2: Country Justice at the Other End" *Rural Heritage* August/September 2022, pp. 26–28.

"Our Auctioneers — Poets, Salesmen, and Philoosophers" *Rural Heritage* October/November 2022, pp. 26–31.

"Irony at the Auction" *Rural Heritage* December 2022/January 2023, pp. 20–24.

"Seeing the Pain of Animals with a Child's and with an Adult Eyes" *Rural Heritage* February/March 2024, pp. 62–63.

"Among the Animals Part 1: Love, Courage, and Tears" *Rural Heritage* April/May 2022, pp. 42–47.

"Among the Animals Part 2: Toward a Common Creed" *Rural Heritage* April/May 2022, pp. 48–53.

"A Good Horse or a Great Horse?" *Rural Heritage* April/May 2023, pp. 24–29.

"Teamster-Team Bonds" *Rural Heritage* December 2022/January 2023, pp. 26–30.

"The Evolution of a Cowboy" *Rural Heritage* February/March 2024, pp. 56–60.

"Searching for the Sun Through Leaves of Grass: On Animal Power," *Orion, The Magazine of Nature and Culture*, under the title "Horse Power," September 2007, pp. 64–71.

*Teamster-Team Bonds, written by Jacqueline Courteau

Contents

Foreword

When you read this book, you will hear, in your mind's ear, a lucid, authentic, distinctive voice. It is the around-the-campfire voice of a sanctioned old-timer. You are going to be captivated by the voice's rhythm, and awed by its precision, and you will be, without a doubt, amused by its wit and humor. Dick Courteau is going to share anecdotes, musings, and reflections about leading the country life and about your country neighbors' adeptness, the craft of their language, their humility, and their deep respect for others. You will listen, to tempt you but with a few vignettes, to the psychological insights of horse country auctioneers, and to the wisdom and mercy of one-armed country judges. You are going to encounter first-person accounts of the scrappiness of rodeo saddle-bronc riders, and of family Homeric cross-country travels in a covered wagon amidst the vertigo of automobiles. You may even get practical advice along the way, in case you are in dire need of acquiring teamster skills. Horses will fall in love in this book, but no, cows will not be jumping over the moon. Cows will leap out of small unbarred barn windows. And so they should.

My fellow reader, even if you are, like me, an unredeemable city slicker who cannot tell apart a breeching ring from an engagement one, when you hear Dick Courteau's voice you will agree that *Profoundly Country* cannot help but being, above all, profoundly human.

—Antxon Olarrea
Professor Emeritus
The University of Arizona

Introduction

The purpose of this collection of essays is not only to entertain but to provide fodder for reflection or memory, nostalgic memory, perhaps, for my older readers. These essays relate part of the story of my life, during these last 90 years, over a wide and varied swath of rural America as I journeyed from place to place and job to job. So they are somewhat autobiographical, but they are not intended to tell my personal story but to reveal, by providing glimpses into that story, a representative picture of rural life and work during these past nine-tenths of a century, a picture that must seem distant and foreign to younger readers.

Part 1 includes 22 essays that have been published in past issues of the magazine *Rural Heritage*, including one by my guest writer, my daughter Jacqueline, who tells a beautiful story about me and Della the injured mare. Several of these articles were adapted from the "Angle From the Mountain" column that I wrote for our local bi-weekly in Elkins, Arkansas, the *White River Valley News*—now defunct, sadly, like so many of our small newspapers.

Part 2 includes two essays that cover similar themes but differ in tone and length from the *Rural Heritage* essays. "A Taste for the Ozarks" is a brief memoir of my time in Arkansas. The longer and more academic piece, "Searching for the Sun Through Leaves of Grass: On Animal Power," was published in condensed form by *Orion, The Magazine of Nature and Culture*, under the title "Horse Power" in September 2007.

In compiling this collection, I first attempted to thread these essays into some kind of narrative, but I soon discovered, after some frustration, that the effort was in vain, that such a narrative would impose upon the stories a false coherence. Each was written as an autonomous piece, and the best I could do was to organize them into broadly related groups. Read them in any order you please.

Part 1

Writings from *Rural Heritage*

The Good Life

Where is the good life? Everyone wants one, but where is it? Broadly speaking you can lead a rural life or an urban life, country or city, but where is the good life? Poets and philosophers, as well as we, the common people, have been arguing this question for thousands of years.

Some 40 years ago, at the height of the back-to-the-land movement, I met a young man, Mike Cosgrove, who had been raised in the huge metropolis of Houston, Texas, but had moved to a small farm in rural Arkansas. Mike, thirty-ish, was a homespun philosopher, and a very amusing wit. Sitting on my porch one day, I posed the question to him. "Mike," I said, "ever since the days of the Roman poets and down through the ages to our own Wendell Berry, writers and thinkers and common people have been pondering, 'Where is the good life, in the city or the country?'"

"Oh," Mike replied, "there's no question about it. The good life is in the city. It's just that some of us like a bad life."

So—just chalk me up as a lover of the bad life. That's right. For many of us, the "bad life" of the country is really the good life, the richest in experience and the most satisfying. I'm speaking of a life working with cattle and horses, or maybe raising free-range hogs or chickens or growing some crop or a garden, a life where you dirty your hands and talk to your neighbors.

In my many long years on this planet, so many of the earlier ones spent as a nomad, I have participated in a wide variety of the multitude of phases of rural life and work. As a child and teenager I milked cows, forked manure, and slopped hogs in Minnesota, and for a short time cut pulpwood by hand in the far northern woods. I have driven tractors in the fields of North Dakota, stacked loose hay with a pitchfork, old-style, in four northern states, and ridden for cows in Montana, Wyoming, California, and Texas.

Throughout all, the driving force in my life has been the horse. I'm not sure why. Maybe it's in the DNA. Certainly, I was deeply impressed by earliest childhood memories. During my toddler years, I lived with my mother, little brother, and older sister in an old farm house along the gravel road leading north from Little Falls, Minnesota, to Camp Ripley, six or eight miles further on. Sitting in the yard one summer's day, playing in the dirt, I looked up and saw a wagon pulled by horses with arched necks and flowing manes, followed by two or three mounted soldiers.

Years later, when I asked my mother about that memory, she exclaimed, "My God, Dick! You were only nine months old

when that happened!" I must have been a little older, but at any rate, we moved from that house when I was three, and that clear memory, that image, has remained indelibly imprinted on my mind's eye for some 85 years.

Another childhood image remains strongly imprinted there. It was at the semi-abandoned Rekstad farm, where I lived briefly with foster parents. I was standing near the ruins of an old log barn, watching some stray cows in an unfenced stubble field to the north. Suddenly a boy—he must have been somewhere in his teens—came swooping in at a gallop on a small horse, and, riding in a tight circle around them, he gathered up those cows and took them down the dusty road. Heightening the drama, and firing my seven-year-old imagination, was the fact that I never learned where that boy had come from nor where he went with those cows.

A very few years later, I, too, was on a horse's back, and was to spend much of my life there until the age of 83. I spent four rodeo seasons riding saddle broncs and bulls in the days of the original Rodeo Cowboys Association (precursor of the modern Professional Rodeo Cowboys' Association) and I've broke and trained horses to the saddle and harness in Montana, Nebraska, and Arkansas, though the roughest ride I ever took outside the arena was in Virginia, that enchanting southern state where much of the West began. Finally, I acquired a little livestock farm in the Ozarks and ran a nearby cattle farm for absentee owners.

I skip through these glimpses of a gypsy-like rural life on the land not to write an autobiography but to introduce myself and to suggest that I might have a few things of common interest to relate. While much of this country work has been hard, dirty, and dangerous, there has been a lot of excitement and drama too, and long, contemplative times of intense but quiet interest. And there's been more than a little humor.

Country life for most of us has meant a life with animals. The lives of animals, domestic or wild, are fascinating in themselves, but the lives of our farm animals are doubly so because they are so closely interwoven with our own. I would like the opportunity to visit with you, the readers of *Rural Heritage*, about some of the aspects of our life out here in the "rurals," most especially to relate a few anecdotes from my life with animals over the past many years.

Our chats won't be exclusively about animals, though. Our rural life is more than our animals and our technology and our practices, more than wagon wheels, walking plows, and when to plant corn or mow hay. We have a rural culture, too, our particular vocabulary and figures of speech, and a poetry rooted in rural life, like that of the Scottish Robert Burns and our own Robert Frost and others. We have humor and a few jokes all our own, and the stand-up palaver of our colorful auctioneers, and I'll touch upon some of that. What we don't have are very good ways of exchanging ideas, especially opposing ideas, like about the environment, climate change, animal welfare—subjects that might provoke controversy. We have to work on ways of friendly disagreement, and I'll be dropping an occasional good-humored opinion, but mostly I'll just be having fun talking about life on the land, your land and my land, this land that we all share together.

If there is such a thing as being "professionally country," I guess that term would apply to me. My life has been lived mostly in what my wife calls "the rurals," engaged in rural pursuits, and my few published writings have all been about horses and donkeys and related subjects. During the several years I spent in the city, teaching Spanish, the goal was always just to save enough money to acquire a little farm and get back to living on the land.

I wasn't born in the country, though. At age six I was taken, along with my four-year-old brother Rolly—we were by then foster children—from the small city of Little Falls out to the large Nelson farm there in Morrison County, 100 and some miles north of Minneapolis. My little brother was assigned, early on, to household chores, but I, being older, was sent to barn and field, where I became immediately enchanted by that world of cows and horses, pigs, chickens, and sheep, and by that still half-wild landscape of rocks and trees and swamps full of cattails and frogs. Ninety years later, I am still enchanted by life away from the bright lights and traffic.

In the essays that follow, I will try to impart to the reader a little of the sense of wonder and excitement that I experienced as I lived and wandered through such a great part of what the Australians would call the "outback" of this great nation.

First published in Rural Heritage *August/September 2021, pp. 52–54.*

Changing Times
in the Boonies

Life and agriculture were changing everywhere in that earlier half of the 20th century, when I first came onto the scene, even in the rougher backwater parts of Minnesota. Modernity was moving in, but the 1800s were hanging on. This duality was exemplified by the very progressive Nelson farm and the contrasting old-style farm of their friends and neighbors, the Waddells. The Nelson farm dominated the landscape of our rural community by its silos and its huge barn, 100 feet long, with its round roof 50 feet high at its peak, where the track was secured that conducted the rope-and-pulley arrangement that lifted the rope slings loaded with loose hay and carried them back into the huge mow, where 100 tons could be stored for winter feeding. The Waddell barn was a low two-room log structure. I can't remember about hay storage, but it must have been outside, in those rounded stacks we used to build that shed water so well.

The Nelson cows were secured within 36 metal stanchions, which enclosed their necks but allowed limited freedom of movement. The Waddells used cow chains (see photos) to tie their half-dozen cows. The Nelson cows drank from automatic drinking cups in front of each stall. The Waddell cows drank from a large round outdoor tank constructed of wooden staves (I'm sure that the daily trip to the tank was a relief from the indoor confinement of those bitter northern winters, and all in all, I would rather have been a Waddell cow.)

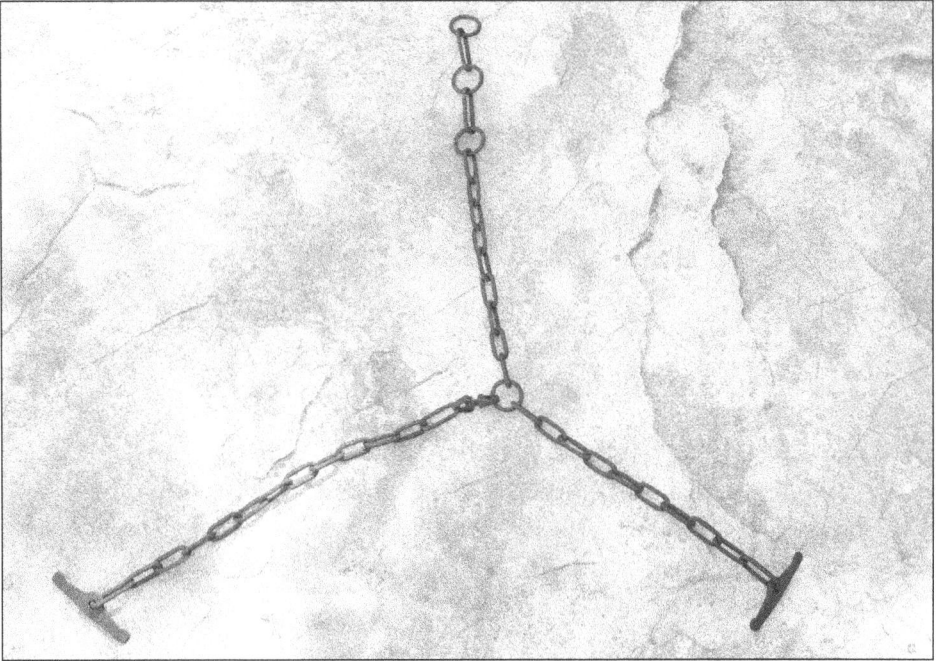

Cow Chains PHOTO: CALEB COURTEAU

The Nelson cows ate alfalfa. The Waddell cows ate meadow hay. The Nelson farm was powered by two modern tractors, supplemented by horses—the Waddell farm by horses alone. I could go on with the contrasts, but my purpose is not to draw a detailed picture of the two individual farms but to portray the life and times of the changing rural America where I was growing up 75 years ago and more.

There were, in our neighborhood—the neighborhood, as I remember, encompassed roughly a three-mile radius—at most four progressive farms, none as imposing as the Nelson farm. Only one, the Waddell farm, stood at the other extreme, almost quaintly alone. A few others, in that rough land, were partial farms, their owners working at outside jobs. Some small farms were being abandoned altogether for high-paying jobs in the city during World War II, while a few others were lying vacant or were becoming residences only. Sound familiar?

So what was life like, in that long-ago time and place? I can only speak for the farm where I was raised, where life seemed like an endless round of choring. All those cows had to be milked twice daily. To feed them, we carried "gunny sacks" (burlap bags) of ground feed on our backs from the granary thirty yards away, and fed them heavy silage in tubs, hand-carried to each cow. Hay was forked to them by hand thrice daily. Buckets of grain and skim milk were carried to the hogs, separately quartered some little distance away. And always there was the cleaning, cleaning, cleaning, of gutters, stall and pens, with pitchfork and shovel.

The end of winter brought a little relief, when most stock was turned out to pasture, but spring also brought the drudgery of picking rocks from many acres of fields with a team and wagon, in that glacial plain where the frost heaved up a new and abundant crop each year (frost was the explanation given).

With June, haying began. We younger children had to stand by as step'n'fetchits, to run for a wrench or hold something in place. A little older—not much older!—we were handed a three-tined fork to help build an outdoor stack or to "lay" the load on the hay wagon as the loader gathered the windrow and dumped it over the rear of the hay rack.

In July or early August came the long days of shocking oats, setting the bundles on end in shocks of eight or ten, with the heads of grain upright and exposed, to ripen evenly before the threshing machine arrived. Those couple of days of threshing were full of camaraderie and were almost festive, as neighbors came with their "bundle teams" of horses and wagons to haul the shocks of grain from the fields in a steady procession to keep the threshing machine running.

Most of the work was not this much fun, and looking back I have often wondered why we had to work so hard, with all that labor-saving machinery in use. I have decided it was because we had all that machinery. To put it in economic terms, our supply side was out of balance with our distribution side. With our modern tractors, and all the accessory machinery for producing feed and fodder, we were able to till enough acreage to support a large quantity of livestock, while at the barn, we were still using methods probably not much changed in a thousand years. We chored with fork and shovel, bucket and bag.

But farm life was not only work. During all those growing-up years, we children were of course attending school, and those one-room schools were fun. The largest attendance we ever had at Districts 85 and 119 (consolidated even then) was fifteen pupils, so we were truly like a large, friendly family. We kids all enjoyed the society of close and trusted friends. And did we have fun! During the three recesses we would keep a game of softball going, or play games like Pom-Pom-Pull-Away or Annie-Annie-Over (or should that be, "Anti-Anti"?).

The small bookrack was popular and well-used, with titles like *Black Beauty* and *Beautiful Joe, Heidi* and *Hans Brinker or the Silver Skates.* After our noon lunch came the magical time when the teacher, from the front of the room, would read another serialized installment from some novel. We listened in rapt attention. The instruction in reading, arithmetic, geography, etc., was excellent.

Social life revolved mostly around the one-room schoolhouse and the church, though in that land of mixed beliefs and disbeliefs, the school was more important. The annual Christmas program provided occasion for socializing by grownups, and for children to show off with their singing and recitations. Especially joyous was the end-of-the-school-year picnic, when parents and children would come together to visit and to play, and to enjoy the great pot-luck lunch. After lunch, there was the fun of outdoor contests like the three-legged race and the wheelbarrow race.

Especially delightful were the pie suppers, to raise a little cash for this or that purpose. The young lady would bring her pie to be sold, then when its turn came, she would stand behind a sheet hung across the front of the room while a gas lantern played her shadow upon the sheet (we never did have electricity in that school). The young men were supposed to have to figure out whose shadow it was they were bidding on, and so with whom they would be eating pie. Truthfully, I think there were few surprises when identities were revealed. I do remember one occasion, though, when the young man had gotten cross-communicated (maybe she had changed skirts?) and had bought, too soon, the wrong pie, and was obliged to make a second purchase and thus be faced with the prospect of eating pie with someone else's friend also. A lot of fun was had at his expense until accounts were settled and the two couples were appropriately squared away.

Of the workings of rural society, the most successful and satisfying was how the young were so smoothly incorporated into the world of adults. We boys, as we entered the teen years, with our new surge of strength and confidence, began working shoulder-to-shoulder with the older men, increasingly as equals. With lots of high-spirited joking and kidding, but serious conversation too, pitching hay onto a wagon or at coffee break, we were drawn into their circle, feeling approval and acceptance, with all the steadying up that that lends during those unstable years. My female peers, in their role, were going through an analogous transition. At least that's what I thought I was watching. Our contemporary women might have a different take on their own history, but there I won't go.

I went back to visit my old country neighborhood a few years ago. Most of the little farmsteads, such as they had been, had disappeared, and just a few large farms seemed to be cultivating all the land worth tilling. Of the long string of buildings on the grand Nelson farm, once connected in an L arrangement to shelter against northwest winds, only the house and the shed protecting the electric well pump remained, both in grave disrepair. I searched and found among the weeds and brush the crumbling foundations of the great red barn. The massive home-constructed silo with its thick rock-and-concrete walls, which had once presided over all like a fortress, had vanished. To the south, all trace of the Waddell farm had disappeared.

Returning home, I passed by my old school yard. The small square concrete pad that had supported the hand pump over the well was still clearly visible. Cows had kept the grass well-cropped all around. Approaching the rise where the white Lutheran church, with its steeple and bell tower, had proudly overlooked that flat countryside, I could see that clumps of tall saplings now belied the existence of any former structure. Across the road, in symbolic irony, the graveyard was well kept.

First published in Rural Heritage *August/September 2021, pp. 52–54.*

PHOTO: CALEB COURTEAU

Dick with son Caleb and daughter Jacqueline at the unoccupied and rundown house on what remains of the Nelson farm in 2023.

Profoundly Country

I have written earlier, in a rather nostalgic vein, of "the good life" out in the country, but in the past few generations the percentage of our nation's population that lead rural lives has dwindled to a tiny fraction. Why? The main reason, of course, is technology—technology and economics. It has simply gotten harder to make a living on the land in modern terms. But it has seemed that, in my lifetime, many farm folks just slipped away, more drawn by the lights of the city than held by the charms of the country. Driving through the little country towns now, one sees a lot of empty stores and boarded-up windows. Some of the tinier towns have all but disappeared. I'm not a socio-economist trying to explain with research and data, why this is so. I'm an old man trying to tell what it has been like to lead a profoundly country life doing so many different kinds of country work and living in such various settings in different states, over so many decades reaching deep into the past century.

At the outset, I might point out that there are many different kinds of work and styles of life in "the rurals." The hog farmers and the chicken farmers lead lives quite distinct from those of the crop farmers. Out West, the cattle ranchers and the sheep ranchers enjoy their own particular ways of life. The loggers are mostly rural dwellers, and the persons who run the farm equipment stores and repair shops and cafés, etc., that live in the little towns and serve the farm and ranch population are also called rural. My focus, though, is more strictly on the farm and ranch life that I have experienced.

My early years, until the age of 16, were spent mostly on the farm of the Nelsons, second generation Norwegians in central Minnesota on what was called a "general farm." We milked 30-some cows, raised hens and sold eggs, and kept a few brood sows and a flock of sheep. We grew the hay and grain to feed everything, partly with horses. Life was an endless round of choring. Tons of manure to load with fork and shovel, hay to pitch, and heavy tubs of silage to carry to the cows. In the spring, many loads of rocks had to be hauled off the newly plowed fields with team and wagon. It was a life of hard physical labor.

One of the things I remember most about that kind of farm life was the grubbiness. It seemed our clothing was always a little

The Nelson Barn PHOTO FROM THE NELSON FAMILY

dirty. The dust from the alfalfa hay being fed in that tight barn would turn the lights brown and make a person choke and cough convulsively. Outside and in the fields, the sticky grease and dust from lubing the tractor, plows, and other machinery would form a patina over the hands.

Despite these little downsides, some of us loved that life in Minnesota, living and working with the animals there amid the little hills and the second-growth forest, between the many swamps with their cattails and rushes and frogs, with the abundant small wildlife all around. For recreation, we could fish or swim in one of the clear lakes everywhere nearby. On Saturday nights, in summer, we could watch from our cars the free movie being shown on the screen set up by local merchants on or near the railroad right-of-way, interrupted only by the whistle and the clattering on the tracks of an occasional passing train.

I might have stayed in that pleasant land, but as a foster child I had no stake in things and I drifted west, alone, starting for the first foray at the early age of 15.

In the wheat fields and beet fields of North Dakota, life was intense during the seasons of tilling, planting, and harvesting, but things got relaxed in winter, with plenty of leisure. Playing cards was a big pastime during those months, whist being the favorite game.

Going farther west, to the ranching country of Montana, I again found a life more relaxed than the busy life of the Minnesota farm with its multiple animal enterprises.

Gyspying then down to the big cow country of northern Texas and later across the Southwest to California, I again found life to be less arduous. On the big ranch north of Amarillo where I spent my 18th winter, we had a team of mules, Bingo and Jitterbug, that pulled a wooden-wheeled wagon which we used to haul hay to two large herds of young steers and replacement heifers pastured along the Canadian River bottom. In the afternoon, we would each take a saddle horse (there were two of us) and ride to the big outlying pastures on higher ground where we would spread range cubes (cubes they were called, but they were actually small cylindrical blocks of compacted protein) on the grass to large bunches of cattle. We were always finished with our work by mid-afternoon and back to the cabin and corral that we called "cow camp."

At the California ranch where I further drifted in a couple of years, the work was even lighter. I would arise before dawn, saddle up and ride to check on the three windmills pumping water to three huge stock tanks, and my workday would be over by noon, except for one day a week when, with the single horse at my disposal, I gathered heavily pregnant heifers ("springers") for shipping to dairies in the Central Valley.

Undoubtedly, those most attached to their way of life were the cattle ranchers and their sons and daughters. Chasing a cow on a horse is a lot more fun than milking her in a stuffy barn. And it wasn't just the men and boys who were having all the fun. The cowgirl is not a figment of the Hollywood imagination and country music. At the Branger ranch in Montana (about 600 cows) and the even larger neighboring ranch that held their brandings together with the Brangers as a cooperative affair, with good food and an air of celebration, it was the women and girls who roped the calves and dragged them to the fire for their branding, shots, and all. Of the half dozen of those females who took part, the oldest was in her thirties and the youngest only about twelve, maybe a little younger. And they were pretty good ropers, too, some of those girls—a lot better than I, who have always been a miserable roper. They roped and we young men wrestled the calves on the ground.

So there were the upsides and the downsides of country work and living. There were the festive brandings and the Saturday night dances. Some of the jobs provided lots of ease and leisure while on others, the work was hard and the hours long. The nature of the work and much of the lifestyle depended, of course, on the kind of enterprise—cattle ranching, dairy farming, etc.—but also on the individual employer, and oh! how they could vary! On some of those jobs you were with the same person in the same place 24/7. It was almost like a marriage, in that one's satisfaction and happiness could depend on a single individual.

The dairy farmers, it seemed to me, had drawn a dreary lot. Those cows have to be milked twice a day, seven days a week. It's a regimen that can be stultifying. A common saying in my youth was: "All work and no play makes Jack a dull boy." On one occasion during our trip with the covered wagon through Kansas and Nebraska, a young dairy farmer saw us passing and quickly saddled his little pinto horse to gallop down from his barn and overtake us, to share, if ever so slightly, in our adventure. But he didn't know what to say or do, and he soon galloped back.

One of the downsides of country work was the danger. Agriculture has become highly mechanized and those machines have made agriculture one of the most dangerous occupations in America. (Rodeo, which emerged from ranching, is probably the nation's most dangerous sport. A cowboy choosing to get into bronc riding or bull riding for the long term knew he was almost certain to be injured, it was only when and how badly. But deaths were rare. When you heard of a cowboy who hadn't returned since the last season you would ask, apprehensive of your own fate, "What! Did he get killed in some early show? Like Denver? Some bull get him in California?" The answer was almost always that no, it was a car accident or a crash in some light plane going between rodeos. One of the tall, blond Templeton brothers, a top-notch bronc rider of impressive build and appearance, had been killed over the winter in a sawmill accident. The bull rider telling about Templeton's death commented, "That metal kills.")

Just within my narrow neighborhood in Minnesota, I knew, during my brief childhood, of three terrible accidents, two of them fatal. In one case, a farmer fell into a threshing machine and died beneath the knives that, thrusting up and down, slashed the twines that bound the bundles of oats as they passed into the machine. In another case, a farmer got his arm caught in a corn picker. I was too young to know, or am too old to remember, how serious was his injury, but it was bad. A young man who lived only a couple of miles away, one of the Johnson brothers, died of head injuries received while earlier helping to feed firewood to a belt driven buzz saw. More recently, here in Arkansas, a local farrier, an acquaintance of mine, was killed when a tractor rolled over. I myself am no stranger to farm accidents. At the age of 17, the power-take-off of a big Farmall M tractor caught my pant leg and snatched me down and wedged me between the drive shaft and a parallel metal beam. There is no good medical explanation for why I'm alive and writing about it.

Those machines can be not only dangerous, they can be slave drivers. Going north with our covered wagon in 1981, we camped in northern Kansas in Decatur County, in an area tilled mostly by farmers of German extraction. Among the group that came to sit by our campfire that evening, a past-middle-aged farmer related how, back when they were farming with horses, the horses had to be rested and the teamsters could go to town in the evenings and play ball. When the tractors arrived on the fields, with their inexhaustible energy and their headlights, the farmers worked into the night. In the fall of 1950, I myself was hired to operate a sugar beet topper in North Dakota from midnight till noon, while my partner ran the machine in the field the other half of the day.

In areas of all-purpose farming, like the part of Minnesota where I spent my early years, the new machines seemed to bring with them a kind of feedback loop. With the powerful tractors, more farming could be done with fewer hands, so the farms grew larger and the extra manpower went to the city. With the new machines, one person could grow the feed to support more livestock, while at the barns, the choring to care for that livestock was still done by traditional manual labor. So there was an imbalance—machines on one side now, human hands on the other, and the remaining workers worked harder than ever.

An oft-repeated saying among farmers in my day was, "The more you do, the more you have to do." Quite related is another maxim quoted often by Maeve's father, the late Captain Robert Dolan: "You can't just do one thing."

A couple of years after that California job riding windmills, I landed, in my early twenties, on a modern "progressive" ranch on the large Crow Indian reservation in Montana run by the white, non-Indian Tuggle family. That's right, folks, within the reservation. One of the injustices in America has been that, having taken from the natives the lands they had roamed and confined them on reservations, the government then opened those reservations for lease, to be exploited by their European conquerors.

(I have used the term "progressive." By progressive I mean not only the use of the new machinery but the employment of the non-traditional practices or devices that force production, such as artificial insemination or an accelerated calving schedule. I do not disapprove of all these things. I merely define the term.)

The Tuggle ranch farmed the rich northern slopes of the Pryor Mountains with a D-6 Caterpillar tractor. This technologically progressive ranch, toward the western edge of the reservation, had built a large calving shed so they could calve out the cows months before the normal calving season in that northern land. This gave them an economic edge, since the calves would be heavier and bring more dollars at sale time in the fall, but it was at the cost of much extra labor, as we worked under lights to birth those cows and the next day had to bed down that shed with straw and clean out the droppings. The ranch also raised hogs and sheep. We worked all the time.

I quit this job during spring fencing in a huff with my autocratic employer and went to work for a Crow Indian matron who held tribal rights deep within the same reservation but quite a few miles away, along Beauvais Creek, named during French tenure. Hers was a more traditional pastoral practice. Presiding over somewhere between 100 and 200 cows, I was to ride and watch and aid in difficult births (there were few that I can remember). I had to rope the newborn calves, vaccinate, castrate, apply de-horn paste and ear-mark them in order to identify ownership among my matriarch's family members.

Nature was my mistress. As spring turned into summer, I had to arise ever more early, before sunrise, or the cows would be "brushed up" along the creek, but my work was almost always finished by noon, after which I had time to read a novel or Greek philosophy or study Spanish.

How had I been able to land these cushy riding jobs? Well, not everyone likes riding a horse, and few can withstand that kind of isolation. On the reservation job, I might not see another human for a couple of weeks.

The great disparities in workload in the jobs I have described were due mostly, of course, to the fact that ranching requires far less labor than farming. The grazing industry is famous for the few workers needed to tend large herds. In another great pastoral country, Argentina, the eminent writer, D.F. Sarmiento, put it this way: "Mientras más cabezas hay menos manos ocupan." (The more head [of cattle] there are, the fewer hands kept busy.)

Grubbiness, hard work and long hours, danger—these were all qualities of life that we shared with our working-class city cousins. One downside of country living more remarkable out here than in the city was the frequent solitude. This varied greatly from place to place and from region to region. The effects were probably worse on the women, who so often have been confined indoors at domestic work without social stimulation. The writer Kurt Vonnegut declared that women simply need more people in their lives than men. Laura Ingalls Wilder, in one of her series of books, the one entitled *These Happy Golden*

Years, writes of a woman who was stricken with mental illness during a long period of isolation near DeSmet, South Dakota, in the late 1800s. On the three large cattle ranches that I experienced during my Western years, in three states (Montana, Texas, and Arizona), that operated land extensive enough to require cow camps, management had employed husband-and-wife teams, besides a single cowboy, presumably for stability.

Country people have traditionally done a lot of reading—those who could read—to combat the solitariness and cultural deprivation. The cowboys of the West, in the "old days," reportedly read a lot and would ride long distances to return with their saddlebags full of books. One Minnesota farm wife was reading the works of John Steinbeck when I knew her. I myself have always read a lot. A farm wife in North Dakota wrote poetry about progress (Oh, those new combines!). It was amateur stuff but she was trying.

By far the most lively of the social and cultural activity in my rural life took place at the tiny village of Roscoe, Montana. The multiple branches of the Swiss immigrant family, the Brangers, kept a square-dance club going. After Saturday-night dances everyone would gather for gossip or political talk at one or the other of the two bars that, along with the post office, a small general store, and an automobile repair shop, constituted the entire village.

The only downside I saw to this delightful community is that we did too much drinking. And there were occasional fights.

Life at Roscoe, Montana, was more like what I have come to imagine as European village life than anywhere else in my experience.

Looking back on a long life of 90 years spent almost entirely in rural settings, doing widely varying farm and ranch work all around the country, I am struck by the observation that the more progressive the farm or ranch and the more labor-saving stuff we had, the harder we had to work. At the Nelson farm in Minnesota, we had two tractors, a full line of machinery for haying and for row crops, a milking machine, an electrically powered machine to unload silage from the silo, an electrically powered machine to clean the gutters in the barn, a silage cutter and a tractor-powered belt-driven feed grinder, and various lesser machines like the cream separator and a fanning mill. We arose early and usually didn't finish our work until about 8:30 p.m. On the big Texas cattle ranch where I cowboyed later, we had two mules, four saddle horses, and a wagon. We cared for several hundred head and typically finished work by mid-afternoon. Of course, the vast difference was the result of one being a farming operation and the other grazing. I merely point out the effect upon the workers of the different kinds of rural enterprise.

I might have drawn a different comparison—between two different farms. A mile away from the Nelson farm, which was operating there on the cutting edge of the newly developing industrial agriculture, was the Waddell farm, trudging out of the 19th century, powered by three Belgian horses. The half-dozen Guernsey milk cows provided most of the family income, supplemented only by Oswald Waddell's small part-time job driving us seven or eight children in his 1930s van from School District 119 to District 85, two miles away, with which it had consolidated.

The Waddell cows were kept well-groomed in winter. The Nelson cows were well fed and well housed in that frigid climate, and some attempt was made to groom them, but the itchy body-oil-and-dust mixture would accumulate on their backs throughout the five winter months that their heads were confined in metal stanchions. The Nelsons were conscientious herdsmen too. They just had too many animals on their modern farm to be able to care for them in a personal way.

Getting back to my own story, I eventually wound up, with my family, in the beautiful, historic state of Virginia, teaching Spanish and running for a couple of years a rented cattle farm. From there I went to Arkansas, where my first wife, the brilliant scholar Joanna Wojtowicz Courteau, had been offered a professorship at the University in Fayetteville. We purchased a middle-sized farm in a rugged corner of the Ozarks where I ran a little herd of mother cows, broke a few horses and taught horseback riding during summers, and pursued other country enterprises like market gardening, brush hogging, building fence, and logging our farm. In 1980, exhausted by a scorching drought and financial insecurity, I decided, with my second wife Maeve, to seek more regular employment. We headed west, to the cowboy country I had found so exciting when I was younger (I was now 47). In view of my considerable experience with cattle and horses, including managing our own farm, I was hoping I might find a stable job in ranching country, possibly one with responsibilities of management. When we arrived at North Platte, Nebraska, I was referred to a rancher up in the Sandhills. This pleasant young man, somewhere in his thirties, was straightforward in his interview. His was not a large operation as Western outfits go, he said, but his multi-faceted operation was too big for one man. He ran a beef herd and he milked cows. He put up lots of hay and he grew irrigated corn. The work began early in the morning and ended, usually, about 7:30 p.m. "And it ain't gonna get much better," he added. But the pay was very good.

I thanked him for his frankness and asked for overnight to consider. Then I returned to the ramshackle house we had rented, along with its primitive little barn, small pasture, and corral. There I could take in a few horses to break and we could raise a large garden for our family. We could keep our rag-tag flock of chickens and the milk goats we would soon acquire. We could fatten a hog.

Thinking hard to make my choice, I remembered all that machinery parked around the rancher's buildings up in the Sandhills. I had learned that whenever you saw that much labor-saving equipment on a farm or ranch, you were looking at a lot of work and long hours. I hadn't come to the West, the scene of my younger cowboy days, to run farm machinery. So I chose the other job that had been offered to me, 40-hours-a-week driving a gravel truck and working at manual labor on the Lincoln County road crew. After my nine-to-five job and on weekends, I could train my horses and care for the other farm animals, work I loved.

Thousands have made the same hard bargain with themselves and settled upon the same compromise—a steady check from the city to sustain a truly rural life in the country.

First published in Rural Heritage, *October/November 2023, pp. 26–31.*

Rural Life Hard But Good: *It Takes Perseverance and Ingenuity*

Author's note: This piece is adapted from three columns that I wrote back in 2010, for a now-defunct local newspaper called the White River Valley News. *Though time has passed, the perseverance of rural folk continues.*

When I settled on Pinnacle Mountain in Madison County, Arkansas, in 1967, deep in hillbilly territory, I already had a lot of hard country miles behind me, besides a lot of "book learnin.'" But my education was just getting started.

Life itself, lived anywhere, is an education, but the hills of Arkansas are an especially demanding and instructive teacher. They'll teach you the how-to stuff, like how to file a chainsaw or overhaul an engine, and they'll teach you the human stuff, like humility and deeper respect for others, as you watch the amazing coping skills of your hill-country neighbors, these folks so long regarded by the nation as backward rubes.

This is a good land, these sheltering hills, with their clear springs, their little plots of rich garden soils, and the abundance of all kinds of wood for building and for warmth. The climate is the finest in the nation, neither too hot nor too cold for very long, with four seasons and days in the spring and fall that are paradise itself. But it's a hard land. Most commercial crop farming is out of the question, and large stretches don't even grow good timber. Logging has been the traditional occupation, but logging these steep slopes is hard and dangerous work. Some livestock raising is possible, but not for lovers of ease.

The brush and briars quickly take over your pastures and the rocks and stumps tear up your brush hog. And fencing—that's rough work anywhere, but this is the only place where I've ever had to use an extension ladder to build fence—to go up over a bluff. If you try to chase a cow on horseback she'll give you the slip, quick as a wink, and stand laughing at you from a greenbrier patch. If you fall off your horse you're lucky not to land on a rock. Most folks have to drive out of here a lot, and the roads are long and rough and hard on vehicles.

There's a high population turnover in these hills—apparently there always has been. For they can be a graveyard of dreams, these hills, and the sheer stress of living can break up a marriage. Too often I've seen them come by twos and leave by ones. If you arrive here with grandiose plans you'll soon find yourself trimming your sails and "cutting the cloth to fit the pattern" just to survive. For my part, I soon quit trying to clear all the trees off my 300-plus acres to make Arkansas over in the image of Montana.

And yet, life "on the mountain"—as we say—is richer and more savory than anywhere I have ever lived, and I've lived in the four quarters of the nation. All this adversity breeds a particular character. A bond forms, a kind of brotherhood of the hills among those who stick it out and survive.

Perseverance and "thinking outside the box"

Life out here demands a lot of physical effort, often side by side with others, and there's nothing like struggling shoulder to shoulder to teach respect for the talents and grit of another. What I came to admire even more than the many skills of my neighbors was their tenacity and dogged perseverance, the cheerful refusal to get discouraged by any number of obstacles and setbacks, like the mechanical troubles that would drive folks nuts in an easier land.

My neighbors have a persistent competence with all this technological stuff that has come to dominate the lives of rural dwellers everywhere. The hill folks have been typically portrayed cartoon-style in the media, with a whiskey jug, a mule, and a plow. Maybe they still have the jug, but by the time I arrived here 57 years ago, they were plowing their gardens with a tractor and had traded the farm wagon for a pickup truck.

The Machine Age had already crept into the hollows. Well, those machines can do a lot of great things, but ya' gotta keep 'em runnin'.

Everywhere it's the same, folks have to keep those machines running, but here they'd been poor so long they'd had to learn to do it without money.

My first summer in Arkansas, a neighbor was clearing pastures for me with a brush hog I had just purchased. It was a new model, so the bugs hadn't been worked out yet, and it kept breaking down. Time after time after time it just tore itself apart. I got so discouraged I was about to have a nervous collapse, but my neighbor Charles would just step off the tractor, once again, optimistically eye the mess and say something like, "If we could find a heavy piece of angle iron and...." Well, you get the picture.

Another neighbor, Leonard Vanlandingham, always kept a couple of old trucks to cannibalize for parts to keep his 1948 Ford pickup going, and he found it incomprehensible when I got rid of the solid old 1946 Dodge Dually that had moved my family here from Virginia. I sold that truck for a song, after only the second major breakdown, and Leonard, I think, found that almost immoral. Leonard himself was a tinkerer of local renown. He once took the oil pump from an old Chevrolet, engine mounted it on a wooden block, powered it with an electric motor, and pumped water to his calves.

It was here in Arkansas that I first saw these country-customized mobile homes, where folks take a modest trailer, build a front porch and add a couple of back rooms and there you have it, your own personalized little house with ample room for comfortable living.

Keep in mind that we're talking about the Arkansas of 56 years ago and more. There's been a lot of change—we're a lot more prosperous now. In those days, Arkansas and the South were still emerging from the century of poverty that followed the Civil War. Older folks used to tell me of growing and selling tomatoes for $10 a ton. A ton! Sure, the dollar was worth more then, but not that much! They cut and hewed railroad ties by hand for 50 cents apiece, delivered by horse or mule wagon to buying stations along the White River. To eat they raised a garden, milked a cow, and butchered a hog in the fall.

Economist John Kenneth Galbraith found that as late as 1950 the average annual cash income in some Ozark localities was no more than $300 per family. But poverty, it seems, was the mother of ingenuity. Everywhere else I had lived and worked, when folks needed something, they bought it. Here, more often than not, they made it.

In this almost cashless economy, Ozark folks had learned to make do with what they had. So they built their houses with their own hands out of the native oak. They fashioned hooks for hanging mule harness out of tree limbs shaped just right and made self-closing door fasteners from worn-out plow shovels. In more recent times, they made gate hinges from the leaf springs of junked cars, and air compressors from old refrigerator parts.

Tom Dunaway, the old jack-of-all-trades from whom we bought our farm on Pinnacle Mountain, was justifiably proud of the sliding part, for the action of a rifle, that he had delicately shaped from a piece of scrap metal using only a hand file.

Tom had an unusually keen eye for the possibilities of applying things like old car parts to purposes never intended by their manufacturers. A later generation would call that "thinking outside the box." There seemed to be a lot of thinking outside the box around here.

A prime example would be a pole that held up the roof sheltering the gas pumps at the old Elkins garage across from present-day Harp's, which was operated during its many last years by James Walker and then son Rodney. Instead of supporting that roof from the ground, some rustic architect had suspended it from the air. What other town could boast a landmark like that!

I kind of got into the spirit of things myself. One especially lean winter when my wife Maeve and I were hard up for a vehicle, I took two old junked International pickups of approximately the same model and year and made them into one pretty good machine, with engine parts, body parts, and running gear so thoroughly intermixed that only the chassis and the VIN could determine that truck's legal identity. I carved a wooden frost plug for the engine block out of a locust limb. It all worked great, but there was a title problem, and thereby hangs a merry tale if I can ever get up the nerve to tell it. (How does that statute of limitations go again?)

Rural Life Hard But Good," July/August 2023, pp. 24–25, and *"Rural Ingenuity: Thinking Outside the box,"* October/November 2023, pp. 80–81.

The roof has since been torn down and no photo was available, but this illustration represents very well the suspended roof over Walker's gas pumps.

How Ya Gonna Keep 'em Down on the Farm … When the Horses Get Under the Hood?

By now, readers of these lines must have realized that country life and country ways are the only road for me. My mother's dad, a Polish immigrant, made a bare living, peasant-style, off a small plot of poor land in Wisconsin, raising a few chickens, some ducks and geese, three or four milk cows as I remember, and probably a couple of brood sows. One of my earliest memories is of riding in a sleigh behind his team of horses to a Christmas play at the neighborhood school. My other grandfather, in northern North Dakota, farmed big, really big, with a couple of dozen draft horses or more, until hard drink and a drought too long broke him completely. I myself was raised in Minnesota by full-blooded Norwegians, good farmers who knew no other way of life than milking cows and raising livestock.

I have fond memories of that rural Minnesota community. The endless choring and field work could be pretty dreary to a kid, but there were fun times too. The church sponsored a couple of social gatherings every month, and at the school we children put on little plays and sang songs for all the folks, and we held a really big spring picnic. As they got older, the more "sinful" of the young people went to Saturday night dances at one or the other of a couple of commercial dance halls. Newlyweds were welcomed into married society with a big charivari (pronounced shivaree up there) ending in laughter and lots of coffee and sweets. Each of us, I think, felt ourselves to be a pretty important member of a little society where everybody more or less knew everybody else.

But even as I was growing up, during those few short years of the 1940s, people were moving away and the country was emptying out and that little society was dying. The smaller farmers went first, then larger ones, until a few years ago, when I last visited, there seemed to be only two or three serious farms operating in the whole neighborhood. The school had been torn down and the church was gone, and of the once-prosperous farm where I grew up only the house remained, terribly dilapidated. The foundations of the huge barn and outbuildings lay crumbling in the weeds. Where had the people gone? Some were in the graveyard, of course. But many had gone to the metropolis of the Twin Cities.

Why had they left? Some social and political thinkers maintain they were forced out by governmental policies that favored big farming. And, undoubtedly, all the new regulations and technology and the big new machines made it hard to stay small and survive. But I think that simple personal choice played a big part, too, the restless desire of people everywhere to seek the bright lights and the excitement of the crowd, where things are going on and, especially, where the young can more easily find the longed-for mate. "Eros, the builder of cities," some sage once wrote.

Certainly the automobile was hugely instrumental in the breakdown of rural society. Some years ago, I wrote a song about that. Well, most of a song.

Way back in 1918, some wag composed for the Ford Motor Company a clever jingle that apparently continued in popularity into the 1920s, though it was only a frank promo for Ford automobiles. When in our teens, my friend Jim Gray would try to sing this ditty on our moonlit horseback rides. He only knew a few lines but they were catchy lines and they stayed in the back of my mind throughout the years. I had never known more than a few of the lyrics of this jingle, so awhile back I decided to create a whole new song along the lines of the original, myself. What came out was similar in absurdity but different in message. My song is definitely not a promo for automobiles. Following is my version.

The first four lines are Ford's, the rest is mine.

Sung to a tune something like, but not quite the same as, "Turkey in the Straw," it's one man's view—mine—of what went wrong in country life.

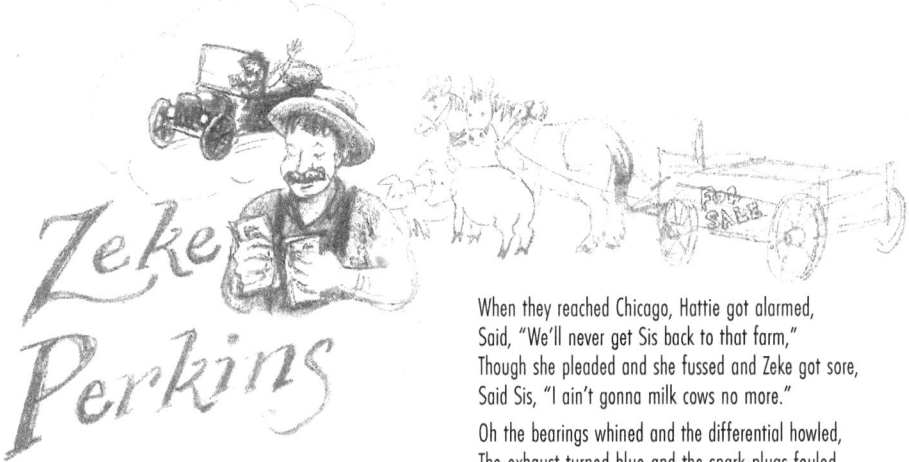

Ol' Zeke Perkins sold his hogs the other day,
The gosh-darn fool threw his money right away,
Went into town a-sittin' on a board
And he came back ridin' in a brand-new Ford.

He came to his gate and he tried to slow 'er down,
He grabbed for the lines and he started in to frown,
Yelled "Hey there Nell and whoa there Bill,"
But the gosh-darn Ford kept a-whizzin' down the hill.

Oh Zeke got worried and his wife began to cry,
But the miles kept comin' and the miles went by,
'round half past noon they reached the county line,
In the wink of an eye they had left it far behind.

Oh the rods began to knock and the valves began to miss,
A tire blew out and the radiator hissed,
They came to a village and his son jumped down,
Said, "So long Dad I like this town."

When they reached Chicago, Hattie got alarmed,
Said, "We'll never get Sis back to that farm,"
Though she pleaded and she fussed and Zeke got sore,
Said Sis, "I ain't gonna milk cows no more."

Oh the bearings whined and the differential howled,
The exhaust turned blue and the spark plugs fouled,
Parts were scarce and gas was high,
Said Zeke, "This Ford was a wonderful buy!"

So he dug a little deeper in his pocket all the time,
Till a leaky radiator took his very last dime,
On a little dusty road they sputtered out of gas,
Hattie cried, "Eureka, Zeke, we're home at last!"

Things are different at Zeke's place now,
He's sold his team and he's sold his plow,
He's out at the elbows and he's over at the heels,
He works two jobs and he cooks the meals,

'Cause Hattie works in the big town too,
So they can have it ready when the payment's due,
But they tell each other, "It's a great life dear,
And you know we're gonna have a new model next year!"

We're gonna have a new model next year.   PHOTO: JOHN COURTEAU

My former newspaper editor, who first read these lyrics, called this song "a good description of the days of early automobiles." Yes, but it was less about the automobiles themselves than about what we did with them, and what they did to us. I know of no mechanical invention ever that has so profoundly rearranged human affairs. The automobile has come to determine where we live, what work we do, who our friends and neighbors are, and even with whom we wind up marrying. Throughout the past several thousand years of history, men and women have lived mostly at the same place as where they worked, which was usually on a small farm or maybe in some village where folks walked to their work in a blacksmith shop, a bakery, a small grocery, etc. Even in more modern times, during my early childhood in the small city of Little Falls, Minnesota, I recall seeing, occasionally, a man walking along the sidewalk or along one of the dusty, yet unpaved streets of the outskirts, carrying his black metal lunch box on his way to work in the lumber yard, the brewery, or the boat works.

In the large spaces of the United States, saddle horses provided transportation for those that had them, which extended the traveler's reach, and the horse and buggy became a popular mode of transportation. The buggy, an American invention, was a specific type of vehicle. Not every horse-drawn conveyance was a buggy. The wagon and the buckboard, for instance, were not buggies. The horse-and-buggy age lasted in the U.S. only about 100 years.

The fact that nearly all transportation was either animal or foot-powered defined the nature and size of neighborhoods. In the part of rural Minnesota where I grew up, a neighborhood was circumscribed within a radius of about three miles. Beyond that, all interactions—of friendship, acquaintance, or commercial exchange—became increasingly diluted. The size of most counties east of the Mississippi was determined by the distance one could drive in a wagon (or buggy, etc.) to the county seat and back in one day.

Henry Ford and the automobile changed all that. Now, according to the Bureau of Transportation, 75% of the U.S. population drives to work. Some 220 million persons spend at least an hour-and-a-half a day in an auto, 3.3 million of them traveling 50 miles or more to work. My personal observation is that many of these drivers seem to be driving to a job that they need so they can pay for the car that they need to drive to that job. Standing on its head the timeworn phrase, Jared Diamond wrote, in his fascinating book *Guns, Germs, and Steel*, "Invention is the mother of necessity."

My Zeke Perkins song may not be fully understood and appreciated by younger readers, who can expect their new Toyota or Honda, their Chevrolet or Ford, to perform well for up to 300,000 miles before they need to acquire another. In my younger days, a Ford, Chevy, or Plymouth would be ready for an overhaul at 60,000.

A used car salesman might assure a prospective buyer that "She burns a white pipe!"—meaning that the engine is sound and that no oil is slipping past the rings nor through the valve guides to be burned incompletely, leaving a trail of blue smoke behind the vehicle and black residue on the tailpipe.

We had a lot of mechanical troubles with those old vehicles in my younger days—and even into my older days. Differentials did howl and then seize up. Transmissions went bad, maybe in just one of the three or four gears. Bearings wore thin and rods knocked or "threw." And the truly terrifying one—tie rods dropped loose, leaving the driver powerless to steer. I have been in three vehicles during my lifetime when this happened, two of them as the driver.

Motor vehicles can be delineators of social or economic class. I used to tell wife Maeve, in our early low-income days, when our old cars and trucks still had generators or voltage regulators that would go bad: Look, Maeve, if you're in the parking lot at Walmart or some supermarket and your car won't start because of a low battery, don't try to hail down the driver of a new Ford or Chevy or a shiny Cadillac. Wait for the old pickup, maybe blowing blue smoke, with a toolbox in the back. That guy will have jumper cables and he'll know how to use them and he'll stick with you until he gets you on the road or maybe takes you to your home.

Maeve hadn't lived out in the hills with me for very long before she was the one carrying the jumper cables and doing the helping out. Life in the hills of Arkansas is a hard but a fast teacher. Life in the rurals anywhere is a demanding teacher. Either you learn or you leave.

P.S. I was amazed the other day when Maeve tracked down the original version of "Old Zeke Perkins." I had thought this bit of commercial doggerel lived on only in myth. Check it out on YouTube. It will keep you smiling.

First published in Rural Heritage *December 2023/January 2024, pp. 10–12.*

My Western Welcome

When we last visited, I was still in my native Minnesota, in the hard-scrabble middle part, trying to make it out of the teen years, but now we must jump to the Beartooth Mountains of Montana, some eight or nine hundred miles away. Minnesota might have held me, for I loved that land in Morrison County, with its fields and meadows and barns, with so much wild land all around, but I had no family ties to the farm where I had grown up and learned to work, had no stake in the claim, no skin in the game. Besides, at the age of nine, I had fallen hopelessly in love with horses, a love which remains undiminished 79 years later, so it was inevitable that I would drift toward cowboy country. Three days after graduating from high school I was on a Greyhound bus heading west.

I was only 16. Though my high-school record had been highly undistinguished, my high performance during earlier, elementary years in a one-room country school had led a wise and kindly teacher, Lucille Olson, to move me a year ahead, casually ignoring pedantic, bureaucratic norms, and I had stayed that one year ahead. Now I was leaving to "seek my fortune."

My first stop was Miles City, Montana, which I knew was in the heart of big cow country. Immediately I started looking for work, trying to talk to ranchers in the bars, which I quickly learned were the social centers of any small town in Montana, almost like clubs. No stockman, though, was eager to hire a greenhorn kid aspiring to be a cowboy. Liquor laws in Montana were pretty relaxed in those days, or at least their enforcement, so the presence of a kid didn't seem to attract attention, and I wasn't trying to buy.

I ran across three Native Americans, but not in any bars. Contrary to our expressed ideals of fair and equal treatment, U.S. law in those days barred Indians from buying alcoholic beverages. I shared my Wonder bread and bologna, and these young men, in their twenties—two from the Crow tribe and one Cheyenne—kindly took this green kid under their wing and gave me my first introduction to the West. These guys engaged in the same kind of banter and repartee as the mainstream Americans I had grown up with, but they were very aware of their ethnic identity. They called themselves, and

A welcome from three "Blankets."

other Indians, "blankets." One of them was a bronc rider, whom I was to meet later in a rodeo arena, as I started riding broncs myself. For a few days they were my only connection to the society of humans, and through them I gained the beginnings of an uncertain foothold in this strange new land.

They couldn't find me a job, though, and I was getting very discouraged and beginning to wonder whether this whole adventure hadn't been a huge mistake. After three or four days I could see that nothing was going to happen for me in Miles City. I was losing heart and was lonesome and getting a little scared. My few dollars were dwindling.

I had to make a move. I yearned for the comfort and security of friends and family. I checked in my billfold and saw that I had just enough left to buy a ticket back to Minnesota. I walked across the street to where Greyhound had a ticket office in a hotel, but stopped a few feet short of the counter. The agent looked at me inquiringly, but I hesitated for a long, very long pause. Then I stepped forward and said, "Billings." Billings was 150 miles further west. My bridges were burnt.

On the bus my spirits lifted. Something was happening again. I watched, fascinated, as the exotic landscape rolled by, a landscape I had known only through books and fantasy.

Arriving in Billings, I learned that a carnival was leaving town. I got hired that night to help tear down a ride and load it on a truck. I worked alongside a Black man, and we quickly became comrades. Somewhere in his thirties, he was a quiet, gentle, soft-spoken person. Neither of us had a room to sleep in that night, but I had a cheap, flimsy sleeping bag so we opened it up, lay on the grass, pulled it to our shoulders, and talked about our lives and our dreams. He said he was a preacher. The next morning we parted and never met again, but I had slept beside the first African American I had ever known.

I took a room in a cheap hotel on skid row—a bed, a chair, a water pitcher and basin, and a shared rest room down the hall. I found yard work for several days till a helpful employer got me a lead on a job at a guest ranch. I pounced on it, and was promptly riding in a station wagon with my new employer, heading southwest toward the Beartooth Mountains, the highest in Montana. Suddenly the snow-covered tops of the mountains appeared. To my Minnesota eyes and Midwest sense of distance they seemed to be maybe 5 miles away, but I was told it was 40 or 50. This altered state of perception—and almost of consciousness—continued as we proceeded south and up the valley of the Stillwater River while the mountains closed around us in an other-planetary world of tumbled boulders, rising peaks, and rushing waters, unlike anything I could have imagined.

I had been hired as a chore boy on a guest ranch. My duties were to milk the four cows twice daily, keep the several cabins supplied with firewood and other basics, and just generally be on call. I had a fair amount of leisure time, but one condition of my job was almost unbearably galling—for some inscrutable reason, on this ranch where it was all about riding horses, the chore boy was not allowed to ride. The owners of this ranch, nice people, had been socially prominent in Chicago, and they had certain fixed ideas about rungs on the social ladder and the proper place of persons.

Two cowboys were working at the ranch. They would soon become "dude wranglers" as the tourist season opened and the guests arrived, but now they were breaking a few colts in a couple of round corrals they had just built of lodgepole pine. After my duties I would go to watch and ask the why and what of their procedures. It was clear I was sick to ride.

Suddenly one day, Joe Lowther, the older horseman, turned and said, "You wanna ride this one?" Of course I did.

He and the other cowboy had a colt saddled in the middle of the corral, a two-year-old gelding, pretty and well-put-together but rather small. They had put him through the basic preliminaries from the ground, but he hadn't been ridden and he had lots of "rollers in his nostrils" (that rattling snort).

They held him while I mounted. When they turned him loose he instantly "blew the plug." It was the first time I had ever felt beneath me that violent bucking action when the horse's back arches upward and you're sitting on a peak of rolling, lashing motion, and the head and ears disappear from the rider's view down between the front legs. "He swallowed his tail," the cowboys say, and the metaphor is apt. Somehow I stuck to him.

I don't know whether Joe Lowther pulled strings or just ignored the rules, but he assigned me my own horse for the summer, a three-year-old filly that had been well started but needed some miles put on her to gentle her down. Joe probably ignored the rules. Tall, lean, and powerful, 40 at the time, half Crow Indian, he was an all-around top hand and well aware of his invaluable service to this ranch, and he was not a subservient man.

When Joe first watched me ride the newly assigned filly, his dry comment was, "Dick, you look like a sack of shit on a horse." I was crushed.

Here I must explain that while I had spent countless hours on the backs of horses over the past five years and had learned to stick to those backs like a burr, I had not had a moment's instruction. I did not feel comfortable at any gait, I always lost my stirrups, and the somewhat painful calluses on my seat bones, from sitting with all my weight down hard in the saddle, lasted into my thirties. Someone earlier, less kindly, had commented that I looked bad on a horse. Joe, though, followed his criticism with instruction, and within a week he had transformed my awkward, uncomfortable posture into the easy, graceful seat that has remained unchanged throughout a lifetime in the saddle.

Joe taught me, in a couple of short verbal lessons, how to ride, and years later, at our little school of horsemanship in Arkansas—aided by my junior instructor, my then-young daughter Jacqueline—I passed the knowledge along to some 50 juvenile riders over the course of 4 years. And now, if there are among my readers any young persons—or older ones for that

Left: Before Joe Lowther's advice—a punishing ride.
Right: And after—a firm, graceful, comfortable seat.

matter—who don't have access to instruction, I pass along to you the gift Joe gave to me, the gift of a graceful, comfortable seat on horseback: Your back should be held straight or even arched ever-so-slightly forward. The balls of your feet should press firmly against the stirrups, with your heels pushed well downward, stretching the calves a little. Your weight—this is important!—should be evenly spread from the balls of your feet through your inner thighs, with just a little on your behind.

Besides the advantages of comfort, grace, and stability, you now won't easily lose your stirrups. Practice this posture, this "seat," and after a week's riding you'll hardly be able to force yourself to go back to your old, natural way. Doing what come naturally is almost always 100 percent wrong.

There is much more to learn about riding, like how to hold your elbows and hands, the touch and feel of your horse's mouth through the reins, etc. Excellence in horsemanship is a lifelong pursuit, requiring, at its best, exquisite skill and vast knowledge, but we won't go further into that. (Read! Many volumes have been published. A good place to start would be Charles Ball's *Saddle Up*, published 50 years ago under the auspices of the *Farm Journal.*) My object here is to point out the effectiveness, the necessity, of instruction in whatever endeavor. A Cuban friend once remarked to me (translating): "It takes training even to be a 'dandy.'"

The few lessons under Joe Lowther that summer taught me not just how to ride properly, but taught me the indispensability of learning by being taught. Experience is not the best teacher. Experience is the worst teacher. Its lessons take too long and come too late, often too late to save lives. The best example I know of this proposition is the horse collar. To pull a load with animal power, the ox-yoke was employed about 4,000 B.C.E., some 6,000 years ago. It worked fine on cattle. About 2,000 B.C.E., a kind of yoke, a wooden bar, was placed across the necks of horses to pull a chariot, but it didn't work out to pull a load. Not until almost 3,000 years later did the horse collar come into use, the only effective device for harnessing the full power of the horse. Our first clear records of the collar's use, about 800 A.D., are from northern Europe, land of the heavy horse, but even then it is thought to have come in from China. Not a good record for experience!

But experience does have tremendous value—to put your new knowledge and developing skills into practice—again, and again, and again. Just make sure that you have the right template, for it has been said that practice does not make perfect, practice makes permanent.

And oh, by the way! At the end of the summer, the other cowboy at the ranch, Clyde Fahlgren, took me to the amateur Labor Day rodeo at Columbus, Montana, where I won third place in the bareback bronc riding. Two years later I began competing in Rodeo Cowboys Association (professional) rodeos, and out of that experience may come a couple of future stories.

First published in Rural Heritage *October/November 2021, pp. 30–33, (under the title "Cowboys and Indians").*

The Snake
Beneath the Seat

L ife with animals has been interesting always, sometimes amusing, and occasionally instructive in a way that leads to a sort of moral lesson, as in the case of a wicked-bucking bull at Grangeville, Idaho, 67 years ago.

Readers who have become a little acquainted with me know that for four rodeo seasons, during my youth, I rode saddle broncs and bulls in rodeos approved by the old RCA, forerunner of the present-day Professional Rodeo Cowboys' Association. To understand the following tale, one should know a little something of the workings of the sport. And rodeo is just that—a highly competitive sport. It is not a show or an exhibition. Contestants are not paid wages or a salary, but depend on their winnings. If they work for the stock contractor who provides stock for the rodeos, temporarily or as steady employees, that is a separate matter. Contestants are free to jump from one town to another, wherever a rodeo is being produced, to enter in their particular event or events (bronc riding, calf roping, etc.), if they can pay the entry fees. And yes, they do have to pay to compete. In my day, at the small-sized rodeos I entered, the fees were usually 10, 15, or 20 dollars per event. Remember, those were 1950s dollars. So between entry fees and gasoline and bologna sandwiches, we less-accomplished hands who weren't often winning were usually pretty broke.

As for performance, in the rough stock riding events, there is the frequent misconception that the whole point, what makes a winner, is just to stay on the animal's back until the whistle blows. True, you have to make it to the whistle to even stay in the game, but in the saddle bronc and bareback riding, two judges watch closely, one on each side, rating the ride according to how hard the horse bucks, and just as important, how stylish the ride. It is easy to disqualify on a technicality.

In 1954, I had started out the rodeo season in June at Hot Springs, Montana, if memory serves me, and had placed third in the saddle-bronc riding, "placed" meaning among the top four riders, and as third-place winner I had taken 20% of the pot. From Hot Springs I drove west to Kellogg, Idaho, where I rode Hell-to-Set, the stock contractor Joe Kelsey's big rank mare, to again place only third. Hell-to-Set was worthy of her name, and only the day before had bucked off Sammy Spahan, a bold and flashy Indian bronc rider (and a helluva nice guy), so I was hoping to place higher, but it was pointed out that I had "gotten in a storm," had lost control of my own movements and flailed about, so I had lost points on the style part.

Nevertheless, I had won some money and had been building up a small nest egg, enough to head south to the next rodeo, Grangeville, Idaho, prepared to pay my entry fees.

I would have had a little more money, but I was carrying extra baggage. Back in Montana, a certain Zack X had attached himself to me, in a way I still don't understand, when he saw me ride and win money at Hot Springs. Zack was about 40, old for rodeo, and had suddenly appeared, somewhere to the south, among our mostly youthful rodeo society, without history or known connections. He was a shadowy figure, a mystery. I found later that there were those who suspected he was some kind of "law," which I have always doubted, though he did, in horseplay one day, demonstrate amazing skill in self-defense tactics, unusual in those times before martial arts were common. He seemed to know every detail of the rodeo craft and to be wise in all the ways of getting by in our world. He quickly exercised an influence over me as only a confident, competent older man can on a younger.

Zack claimed to be a bull dogger (steer wrestler), though he didn't have a horse. That wasn't unusual, though, for he could borrow a horse for the performance in exchange for a percentage of his winnings.

Zack was waiting for his big chance—weren't we all?—and meanwhile I was carrying us both, all expenses—gas, a couple of nights in a cheap hotel, cold cuts and coffee. So after getting entered in Grangeville, Zack in the dogging and I in broncs and bulls, we were almost broke.

PHOTO FROM THE COURTEAU COLLECTION

The huge gray gelding, Tiger, bucked me off in spectacular fashion.

In Grangeville we camped on the creek running past the rodeo grounds. On the first day, I drew a huge grey gelding in the saddle-bronc riding, which bucked me off in spectacular fashion, so we were hoping Zack would bring in a little grocery money with his steer wrestling.

The next day, Zack took the left side on his borrowed horse, with his hazer on the right and the steer in between. At the signal they all bolted away from the gate and the barrier. The hazer quickly got Zack set up for a perfect drop onto his steer, and the horses, with the two men on their backs and the steer between, both kept running in perfect coordination, but Zack just didn't get down. Later, his hazer, and I and others watching, simply couldn't understand why not. Zack had an explanation, but no one was convinced. It seemed to be just a case of failed nerve, and my disillusionment began.

But we still had another chance. For the third and last day, I had drawn a yellowish-tan bull, rather small for a bucking string, but a rolling twisting devil to ride, the kind that if you got him ridden, you were the winner. The day before he had "ironed out" (bucked off) Buck Boyce only two jumps out of the chute, and Buck was a super-tough bull rider, ranked fourth in the nation at that time.

Performance and judging in the bull riding are a little different from the two bronc riding events. This sport conforms more to the general public's idea of what rodeo is all about—just stay on the bull to the whistle. A lot of bulls don't get ridden, occasionally only a couple in a day, and there's not much style to judge, and often one bull stands so far above the others that if you get that bull ridden you are high in the money.

The rule was that if the rider had not yet hit the ground when the whistle blew—if he was still in the air—it was a qualified ride.

The pot was rich here at Grangeville. First money in bulls would be over five hundred dollars. I lowered myself down on the loose yellow hide, behind the shifting hump, and another

"Settin' high" on Bull No. 4 or "goose-egged"?

cowboy pulled tight my braided rope. I nodded, the gate opened, and I was in the arms of God. The little bull twisted and sunfished and kicked out sideways in his peculiar fashion as I hung on and waited eternally for the whistle. When it blew I was sure I was still in the air and I hit the ground elated. But when the score sheets were pooled later at the office, it turned out that, while one judge had me "settin' high," the other had me "goose-egged." I was crushed, and confess to a tearful breakdown when alone at our camp by the creek.

Sturgis, South Dakota, had been our next destination, but "How we gonna get there?" I asked.

"The credit card," Zack said.

My younger readers, those of you under sixty, may not have heard of the "Oklahoma credit card." The term was coined during *Grapes of Wrath* days, during the great migration west out of the Dust Bowl, when thousands were fleeing natural disaster and desperate poverty. The "Okies" were still, during my teen years, a presence everywhere throughout town and country in California. Many had gotten there, it was said, with the help of an 8-foot, 3/8-inch rubber siphon hose.

"Zack," I said, "I don't steal."

"You're so high and mighty," he said. "Then how we gonna get to Sturgis?"

I fell back, then, on that hackneyed old expression—"Zack," I said, "I wasn't raised that way."

"Neither was I," he said, "but sometimes ya' gotta make exceptions."

I reckon we both had been raised under the same absolute ethical code—you didn't lie, cheat, or steal, and the worst of these was stealing. A moral problem often presented to us children was this: Is it worse to steal a penny or a dollar? The answer was, they are exactly equal, for they are both stealing. But in our heart of hearts we all knew that snitching a few apples from your neighbor's tree was not as bad as stealing his wristwatch, and siphoning a few gallons of gas from a pickup was not like stealing a workman's toolbox and the tools of his trade.

The vehicle we selected to donate to our cause that dark night was a semi-truck pulling a livestock trailer, owned by Red Turner. Red had been a prominent rodeo contestant in his younger days, but now he made his living hauling livestock. He had been one of the judges during this three-day rodeo, but I insist that that had played no part in our choosing his truck. It's just that big trucks in those days were still often powered by gasoline, and Red's truck had two big saddle tanks.

I was carrying in my pickup the necessary devices. Most country people, then and now, have always kept handy a siphon hose and a gas can or two, to transfer gasoline from one vehicle to another, or to a tractor or a small engine, etc. We filled a couple of metal jerry cans.

The next morning, getting ready for the trip to Sturgis, Zack and I walked into a café for coffee. Red Turner stepped off his stool wordlessly and handed me a ten-dollar bill (in adjusted 2021 figures, a hundred-dollar bill). I stammered a thanks. I couldn't pour the gas back in his tank.

It was roughly 800 miles to Sturgis. If you'll do the math, dear reader, you'll know that we had to uncoil the rubber credit card more than once to get there. I didn't have money enough to get entered in Sturgis, just enough to get a cheap hotel. I started to build up another little nest-egg—I don't know how, here memory fails, but I must have gotten a few days' temporary work. I would go down to the pens and watch the bucking stock. I don't know where Zack would go. Back at

Red Turner's unwitting donation.

the hotel, when the livestock was being loaded to leave, I said, "Zack, I'm going up to North Dakota."

"Yeah," he answered, and seemed a little sad, "maybe I'm not so good for some people."

I headed north. I don't know where Zack went, for I never saw nor heard of him again. Wherever he went, he apparently kept traveling a ways on my account. When I next opened my suitcase, my expensive camera was missing—a precious gift from my mother on my graduation from high school.

At Killdeer, North Dakota, a crazy wild saddle bronc crashed, at a dead run, into the high arena fence. As he rolled backwards, I stepped off, unscathed, but was broke again. I found work stacking loose hay with a pitchfork, as it was brought in by a Farmall tractor equipped with a Farmhand front-end loader and a buck rake. My employer was a young farmer struggling to support his wife and first child and to keep the farm bills paid. He was alone in his work and he didn't seem very efficient, and he was so stressed out that one day when our haystack—he had built this one—slid sideways and collapsed, along with our morning's work, he broke down in tears and I pretended not to notice.

After three weeks, our work in the hay was over and I left for Texas and Louisiana, where I found steady but modest success in a long series of small rodeos.

And by the way, the rubber snake of temptation was kept coiled beneath the truck seat, ignored and forgotten. I was buying gas with the haystacking wages now, and have never again "borrowed" so much as another pint of gasoline, nor have I stolen a dime from anyone, neither by credit nor loan.

I have had nearly 70 years to ponder the condensed experience of those few weeks. First, Grangeville—here there is mystery wrapped in mystery. Had I really hit the ground when the whistle blew, or should I have rightfully won the bull riding? And Red Turner—which judge was he and why did he give me those ten dollars? Was he the one who had disqualified me and maybe he thought he had made a mistake? Or maybe he felt bad about having to do it, to mark me zero? Or was he the judge that had marked me high and felt that the other judge had been mistaken and thus wronged me? Or was it just that he, an old rodeo hand himself, just wanted to help out a younger man having some really hard luck? In 67 years, I haven't been able to puzzle this one out.

I used to wonder how could I—with such a firm and lifelong moral base—how could I have resorted to that siphon hose, just to travel a few more miles down the road? Reflecting, and watching over the years the same forces at play in others, I realize it's that ambition gets its grip on us. Ambition, which drives us on to personal achievement and sometimes very fine things, can also lead us to selfish pursuits and down a slippery moral slope. Those who passionately follow some dream are most susceptible. Reaching our exalted goal becomes the end that justifies the means, and we lose sight of—or abandon—our values and priorities.

In my case, it was that next rodeo that I just had to reach and win—it was so important!—so I caved in and used the rubber hose. In another instance, a friend just had to keep getting her horse to the next race, so she borrowed money from family and friends, money she couldn't pay back. A professor I knew, at a major university, secretly "borrowed" his office mate's notes, to mine ideas for his own forthcoming lectures, which he apparently considered important in his career. Ambition, in my experience, can work its insidious way at any level—street or university hall.

I remember with warm satisfaction those three hot, sweaty weeks in the Dakota hayfields, and the few days' companionship with that harried young farmer, when I was able, if only briefly, to lighten his load. When I think of Red Turner handing me those big 1950s dollars, with his gas in my tank, I shrink within my pride.

First published in Rural Heritage *February/March 2022, pp. 56–61.*

Just Because
You've Done It Before …

Author's note: Well, readers, here's another story from my days in the sport of rodeo many years ago. I know that riding broncs and bulls and wrestling steers is a long way from the everyday country practices that most of us engage in, but I point out that rodeo is the only major sport in this nation to grow directly out of our work in field and pasture. The following tale, by the way, is true and factual in every essential detail.

Joaquín Sánchez had watched a lot of bucking-horse rides. He had ridden saddle broncs and bulls himself and by now had become one of the three or four best-known rodeo clowns and bull baiters in the nation. So that day up there at Lethbridge, Alberta, when I jumped down off the pickup man's horse and headed back toward the chutes unbuckling my chaps, and Joaquín strode up and greeted me enthusiastically with, "My God, Dick, I thought you were Casey Tibbs," it was the highest compliment I had ever been paid. Evidently, I had turned in a flashy ride on a rough horse and I felt a surge of pride.

The story around that ride begins a few weeks earlier down in Montana, and it ends a short while later, again south of that northern border.

Northwest Montana is a mountainous country, with small-to medium-sized farms and ranches sandwiched between large reserves of government land. In the spring of 1955, working out of a borrowed set of corrals north of Hot Springs, I was finishing up the last of a few colts I had taken in to break. I saddled one of the two remaining horses and, leading the other, rode the fifteen miles or so to visit my friend, Bill "Wild Horse" Haynes.

Bill, almost twice my age (21 at the time), lived and ranched, with his wife Fay, on the gentle slope of a low mountain somewhere between Hot Springs and the town of Ronan. They ran a small herd of mother cows while Fay, pretty daughter of immigrant Romanian sheep ranchers, had her own business raising registered Half-Arabians on government land. Bill supplemented their income by trading horses and helping with the Half-Arabs.

When I arrived that day, he was raking hay with the high-wheeled dump rake. As he pulled up his team and I dismounted, I could see that—trader that he was—he was working a new pair. The near horse, a light-colored dappled gray gelding, showed Percheron blood, while the off horse, a rich bay gelding, also revealed lots of draft horse. From their clean limbs and tight muscling, you could also see the strong strains of light-horse breeding, very likely passed down from the U.S. Army's Remount stallions, which had contributed so much in those days to the gene pool of the horse population of the West.

They were a classy pair, but champing at the bit and rarin' to go, and they looked pretty green in the harness. I was surprised that Bill had hitched them so soon to a dangerous implement like the dump rake, but I guess they hadn't called him "Wild Horse" for nothing.

Bill hired me to drive the two for a couple of days in the hayfield. They were gentle enough to harness and hitch and though they started off pretty rambunctious, they settled down after a few rounds, and I raked up that light prairie hay most of the next couple of days at a slow trot. That tough pair never drew a long breath.

Bill had some kind of an occasional working relationship with Bud Lake, a prominent rancher in the area and a partner in the Zumwalt and Lake rodeo company, among the foremost of rodeo producers based in Montana at that time. Among his services, Bill scouted for new bucking horses. Rodeo horses can quit bucking, and producers are always on the lookout for replacements. As a young bronc rider on the upswing, I was always looking for a chance to practice, so when I said, "Hey Bill, why don't we try these two out?" Bill, always scouting, was ready and willing. The bay and the gray were prime prospects.

It might shock the reader that I would propose a career in rodeo for these two animals that had just worked dutifully in the hayfield. Isn't rodeo a cruel sport? Quite the contrary. If they could qualify as rodeo performers, these two would be treated kindly and receive the best of care, and they would work only a few intervals per week of a few seconds each.

It might also be surprising that horses broke to the harness would be considered as bucking horse prospects. Again, quite the contrary. Many of the great old performers were quite gentle. Some had had experience in the harness, or occasionally under a rider or pack saddle. The roughest ride I ever took in a private corral was on a huge five-year-old thoroughbred gelding in Rockbridge County, Virginia, that you could lead around by the forelock—if you could reach it.

Wild horses usually didn't make the best buckers. For one thing, the truly wild horses, feral mustangs, would be too small. In bucking, as in boxing, it's weight and muscle that deliver the knockout punch. So it was no accident that a lot of the good bucking horses back then carried draft horse blood, and that many of them came from the Dakotas and eastern Montana, or from the prairie provinces of Canada, places where there had been a lot of farming. A really wild horse might be terrified and waste its energy fighting the chute and wear itself out before the ride, or it might simply panic and run headlong into the high arena fence. It was said that the burnout rate was high among the wild ones, that they might buck maniacally for a time or two and then quit.

The gray and the bay, though, they would be cool.

The neighboring Darlington ranch had a one-chute practice arena. A son, Bob Darlington, twenty-something, was a good amateur bronc rider, "amateur" meaning only that he hadn't yet chosen to go pro by joining the Rodeo Cowboys' Association (RCA). We drew lots, and the gray horse fell to Bob, the bay to me. Bob rode first. Whether he managed the gray or bucked off, I can't remember, but I do know that the horse was a strong bucker and "honest." That is, no crazy throwing his head around, no stumbling and falling, no rearing or going over backwards, just high strong jumps, head low between his legs.

The bay horse bucked me off. I was riding very rank horses at that time in my career, but I was riding for the first time my newly acquired Deb Copenhaver Special saddle, and I hadn't yet established my proper length of stirrup, so I "blew" a stirrup, and when you lose a stirrup on a bucking horse, you're usually lost yourself.

It was June and the rodeo season up in that north country was under way and I was anxious to hit the road. I left Bill and Fay and rode back to the corral at Hot Springs, where I finished green-breaking those last two colts and turned them back to their owners, then climbed into my 1941 Packard and headed north to Canada. I arrived at Lethbridge too late to enter the bronc riding, but the rodeo secretary told me they needed an "exhibition" rider.

Now here I'm going to let the reader in on a little of the inside story of rodeo, at least in those long-ago times. By the 1950s, purses had gotten large enough, and transportation fast enough, that some rodeo cowboys—the ones who were earning enough money—would enter two rodeos at a time, schedule permitting, driving or even flying between the two. For instance, one big performance might be on a Saturday afternoon, while the other major rodeo would be in another state that night. Two or more cowboys might charter a light plane and work both rodeos. This could be chancy, and a cowboy might not arrive on time, or not at all. Under the rules of the old RCA, if a cowboy failed to ride his animal out of the chute, if he "turned him out" riderless, he would be barred from competing in that particular rodeo the following year. He could avoid this penalty by paying another cowboy to ride the animal. The alternate rider might be mistakenly announced as the cowboy who had paid the entry fee.

The renowned Casey Tibbs would be paying for my ride. "What'd Casey draw?" I asked the secretary.

"Haynes' Ghost," she replied.

"Haynes' Ghost?" I puzzled, "I didn't know Zumwalt had any Haynes' Ghost," but when she answered, "New horse, big gray," I began to suspect. I strolled over to the pens back of the chutes and sure enough! there he was, my old friend from the hayfield.

I learned that Joaquín Sánchez would be the clown and "bullfighter" here. I had travelled with Joaquín and we were old friends, but I hadn't talked to him since the last rodeo season—cell phones were still far in the future—so he could not know that I was at Lethbridge too. There was no time to look him up. They were loading the chutes.

As I lowered my saddle onto the big gray's back, I could see in his mane just the beginnings of the collar marks, the ruffled mane left by his few days in the harness. He stood quietly. He

I lowered myself into the saddle ...

had known the jingle of harness and the rattle of a hay rake at his heels, and he sure wasn't going to be bothered by my innocent-seeming saddle. The chute boss gave the go-ahead to "pull 'em down" (tighten the cinches) and I could hear the announcer talking about Casey Tibbs coming out of Chute #___ on Haynes' Ghost. But Casey Tibbs was there that day in name only.

It was quite a name, though. Casey Tibbs has been called the greatest bronc rider of all time. These things are hard to prove, but certain it is that Casey was the best-known rodeo cowboy of the 20th century.

I grasped the single buck rein of braided rope, gingerly placed my foot in the right-hand stirrup, and lowered myself into the saddle. From the left side of the chute, another bronc rider held that stirrup and I wiggled in my foot. Everything had to be quiet and calm, so very quiet and calm!

I settled deep into the saddle and gave that fateful nod. I had learned as an amateur not to call out, "Outside!" An old veteran bucker would also have learned that word and might explode while still in the chute.

Strangely enough, I can remember almost nothing of that ride, though it was evidently one of the best of my modest career. I remember only vaguely that the big gray, while powerful, bucked straight and true and he didn't seem especially hard to ride. So when Joaquín burst upon me with an excited, "You must be in the money, Dick! I thought you were Casey Tibbs," all I had in reply was a rueful, "Joaquín, that was just an exhibition ride. For ten bucks!"

The next week, Kalispell, Montana, would celebrate its big Silver Buckle Rodeo and many of us would follow the Zumwalt and Lake livestock south from Lethbridge. What distinguished the Silver Buckle Rodeo was just that—the exceptionally beautiful trophy buckle that was awarded to the winner of each of the five main events. Other rodeos gave buckles, some of the them, but the Kalispell buckle was a little bit special.

I entered the saddle bronc and the bull riding. Bull riding offered an extra chance to make a little money, but it was the saddle bronc riding, years before, that had fixed my sense of identity as a working cowboy. Bull riding and bareback riding demanded their own special set of athletic skills and personal qualities, but saddle bronc riding was more closely related to the challenges that might crop up during the course of a cowboy's work day on a ranch riding fence or riding for cows, and of course, while breaking colts. When I cinched my saddle on a bronc, I felt that I was partaking in the very soul of the West.

The entries in saddle broncs were nearly always fewer. You couldn't really say that saddle bronc riding was more difficult than the other riding events, but it certainly was more complex. On a saddle bronc, there is nothing firm to hang onto, no solidly cinched-down leather bareback rigging on a horse, nor tightly pulled rope encircling the bull, only the floating buck rein and the free-swinging stirrups.

For the first go-round, I drew Quarter to Nine. Quarter to Nine wasn't Zumwalt's top saddle bronc—that would have been Fox. She was probably not even as hard to ride as the huge Snow White or the pinto Pepsi Pete, who bucked with a violent spinning action, both of which I had ridden to the whistle during the past year. But this big bay mare was tall, strong, and dynamic, and if a rider could qualify on her and ride to the whistle, he would almost certainly place among the top contestants.

The mare bucked with me, that first afternoon, in high, powerful arcs, straight along the arena fence. I never felt in danger of becoming unseated, but I failed to get "tapped off" with her, failed to find the harmony of her movements, so it had not been a pretty ride, nor easy, and I was relieved when the whistle blew and the pickup men closed in to take me off the mare's back. When the score sheets were tallied, I had placed third. The mare had been given a high numerical rating because of her flashy performance, but my numbers were low because of my stiff and labored ride. (Horse and rider are rated separately, and the two sets of figures are handed in by each of the two judges and totaled to obtain the composite score for the ride.)

I had placed only third, but the rodeo was just half over, at least for the saddle bronc riders, and I was still in a good position to win. Because of the rather small number of entries in saddle broncs, there would be two go-rounds—that is, each cowboy would ride two horses during this two- or three-day event, and the winner of first-place money and that coveted buckle would be the rider whose numbers for the two rides totaled highest.

For the second go-round, I drew—capricious luck of the draw!—none other than Haynes' Ghost.

Now my chances went way up. Haynes' Ghost? A piece of cake! And my chances got higher as rider after rider either bucked off or otherwise disqualified. As it came my turn, no rider had yet ridden two horses.

I was almost the last to be called, so all I had to do was ride this gray horse that I had so easily mastered last week, and as the only rider to qualify on two horses, 40% of the pot and the buckle would be mine. I didn't even have to risk a fall by loosening up and spurring to win points. I just had to qualify coming out of the chute and then sit down tight and ride him.

I wasn't complacent. How could any rider be complacent, looking down in the chute at 13- or 14-hundred pounds of muscle and bone, standing all aquiver, hot-wired and spring-loaded, ready to slam to the ground any load placed on its back?

Complacent no, but confident I was. Hadn't I just done this before?

I placed my left foot firmly in the seat of the saddle, ready to kick myself upward, outward, and free, should the big horse suddenly "freak out" and dangerously fight the chute, maybe even throwing himself backwards. Haynes' Ghost stood quietly. I then lowered that left foot into the stirrup being held for me, and, seated firmly, gave that solemn nod. The gate swung open. Haynes' Ghost lunged out and bucked me off the second jump out of the chute, the fastest I was ever bucked off in any arena, amateur or RCA.

Rodeo taught us rough-stock riders how to accept disappointment, how to handle failure. In fact, for many of us failure was what rodeo was mostly about. Kalispell had been a bitter disappointment, but Kalispell was behind me now and there were miles and years and a thousand rodeos ahead. Willie Nelson got it right about cowboys:

Always in search of
And one step in back of
Themselves and their slow-movin' dreams.

So I loaded my saddle in the old Packard and headed down to the nightly rodeo at Cody, Wyoming. There I was certain I could do some winning. I had ridden horses lots tougher than those jaded broncs bucking nightly down at Cody. I had done this all before and surely I could do it again. Or could I?

First published in Rural Heritage *February/March 2023, pp. 36–39.*

Don't Give Up

I wrote this verse to recreate, in spirit, the memory of a poem that appeared in a long-ago edition of Country Gentleman.

When the road you're going seems all uphill,

And the spirit flags as the spirit will,

And you're tired and sore and long is the day,

And the goal you seek seems far away,

And the weary spirit cries out to stop,

Rest if you must but don't give up.

For you never can tell how close you are,

You may be near and you may be far,

And you never can tell; with one more try,

You just might pass the goal on by.

So though the spirit cries out to stop,

Rest if you must but don't give up.

The Black Cow
with the Red Eye

In the fall of 1983, having arrived in Lincoln County, Nebraska, only a couple of years earlier, after a journey of 850 miles by covered wagon (but that's another story), my wife Maeve and I were just making a living. I was working on the county roads and breaking a few horses, and Maeve was working at home, raising the kids and growing a garden. To feed our band of horses I mostly just scrounged the fertile roadsides and some railroad land. We were getting by okay, but in this, our catch-as-catch-can domestic economy, we were always on the lookout for a few extra bucks.

Then late that fall the arctic air came surging down out of Canada, making 1983–84 the deadliest winter on the Great Plains in a century. As spring came on, after weeks of facing north winds, cows were simply surrendering to exhaustion and going down, never to rise again.

At the North Platte sale barn one Saturday, hoping to pick up an orphan bottle calf or two, or any bargain that might turn us a profit, I had just stepped back through the door from the café, when Maeve cried urgently from the stands, "They can't get a bid on her, Dick!" Glancing quickly, I saw a thin, black, rough-looking cow on her knees in the ring, much weakened after the terrible winter. "25!" I shouted, and the auctioneer called her off to me.

She was Angus and she was snuffy, but she was almost helpless. I backed my pickup against the loading chute, and by waving a feed sack coaxed her into charging me, on her buckling knees, along the narrow alley. Finally, with one last thrust she charged me up into the pickup and collapsed totally.

We rolled her out of the pickup onto our front yard and covered her with blankets and tarps. We fed her grain from a bucket and brome grass hay, trying to build up her strength. Always, she blew snot and tried to charge us on her crumpled knees. I built an A-frame to lift her up and support her, but she was always on the fight at our approach and her legs kept dangling in the sling. Then one day, after maybe a month, as she hung in the sling during her daily "exercise sessions," legs dangling and moving around helplessly and barely making contact with the ground, I thought, "Maybe this has just become habit." Taking an electric cattle prod (please pardon me, my fellow animal welfarists), I buzzed her. She stiffened her legs and stood.

We turned her out to a small pasture where she prospered on spring grass, but she always had red in her eye as we approached. Maeve and I had hoped to raise calves out of this valiant mother, but our fortunes turned. The man living in the old house we had left in Arkansas was shot and killed, and we had to return to that state. Regretfully, we had to send this feisty black cow, that we kinda admired and had grown fond of, to public auction and almost certainly to slaughter. Which leads me to reflect upon a few lines by the great Persian poet, Omar Khayyam, to whom I was first introduced by a Texas cowboy 70 years ago—

> *Ah Love! could thou and I with Fate conspire,*
> *To grasp this sorry Scheme of Things entire,*
> *Would not we shatter it to bits and then,*
> *Re-mold it nearer to the Heart's Desire!*

First published in Rural Heritage *December 2021/January 2022, pp. 28–29.*

Of Milk You Can't Drink, Horses That Can't Walk, and Crops Gone to Pot

Miracle had died. It had been her third or fourth calving and she was supposed to be providing milk to Maeve's and my increasing brood. We had been trying to get the kids to drink goats' milk, but our goats had been ranging free, which is what goats do unless you have very tight fencing, and they had been eating something that made their milk taste really bad. They had also wandered across the mountain and gotten into our neighbor's ornamentals, which caused problems somewhat more serious than tainted milk. Anyway, Maeve did not even like cooking with the off-tasting stuff, so we were all waiting for Miracle to freshen.

Why the name Miracle? Six or seven years earlier, I had called my veterinarian and said, "This old cow we've been treating, Doc, is going to die. Can I stand by waiting and cut the calf out when it happens?"

He said, "You've done everything you can for that old cow. She ain't gonna make it. You've gotta get that calf out within seconds. Take it now."

I gave the cow a quick and painless death, and with a keenly honed knife, I had in my arms almost instantly a wet calf, snuffling and struggling for breath. The weather being unseasonably cold for mid-March, we took the "Miracle" calf into the house and put her in a toddler's playpen by our woodstove, and started her on goat's milk and milk replacer. Of course, she grew up gentle, and she had given us three or four calves and lots of milk, but now she was dead of a massive and rare infection after calving.

We had three growing children, and to grow kids healthy you need milk. Store-bought milk costs money, and besides, the nearest store was a dozen miles away down a rough dirt road, so we always tried to stay home-grown.

I have rarely heard farmers, even small or near-subsistence farmers, call themselves poor. How can you consider yourself poor when you have cattle, or hogs or chickens, maybe horses, and land to grow food? But cash, now that has always been scarce in the "rurals," so we always tried to have our own milk cow. But now we didn't.

Which brings us to Alvin Diehl. The Alvin Diehls of this nation have always been familiar fixtures out in the countryside. Alvin was a horse trader. More accurately, he was a trader in all things country. If you needed a set of doubletrees or an Oliver 13 walking plow, he might have an Oliver 19—too big—or a Vulcan or a Chattanooga—not your first preference—but he would get you fixed up with something. He was honest and reasonable and he didn't fleece anyone, and he helped keep the wheels of our hillbilly economy greased and rolling.

I'm trying to keep this story on a straight line, but here I can't keep from swerving a little. It was Alvin who once pronounced the eleven words that packed into a nutshell more wisdom about the horse than I have ever heard stated so briefly.

It came about like this. Madison County, my county now for well over a half-century, one of the ruggedest and "hillbilliest" counties of the northern Arkansas Ozarks, is not row-crop country. But one crop it did produce in abundance, back in the days of our hippies and back-to-the-landers, was high-quality cannabis. This kept the county's law enforcement contingent pretty active for several years (and some would claim pretty mellow). A certain David McElyea, an import from a northern state, who acquired notoriety as a grower and a dealer, and subsequent local fame writing of the experience, in his memoir *When Money Grew On Trees,* supplied this (paraphrased) account of his dealings one day with Alvin Diehl. He and his partner considered themselves outlaws (they kinda were). Well, outlaws needed horses, didn't they? They didn't know doodley squat about horses, so they went to see Alvin Diehl. Alvin showed them a horse he thought suitable. "But can he run?" McElyea asked. "Why son," Alvin replied, and then he spoke those eleven words—"They can all run, what they can't all do is walk." What experienced horseperson cannot smile and agree?

But getting back to milk for the kids. I pulled up to the neat Diehl ranch in my pickup. Most farmers and ranchers had stock racks on our pickups in those days. "Alvin," I said, "do you have a cow giving milk?"

"No, I don't have a milk cow right now Dick," he replied.

"Alvin," I said, "I didn't ask did you have a milk cow. I said, 'Do you have a cow giving milk?'"

Alvin grinned. We knew each other. He had bought a few cows on contract for me back when I had more money, and I had broke a horse or two for him, had shod his horses, and had skidded logs for him with my team.

"I have three have had calves last few days," he said.

He saddled his rotund little Quarter Horse mare Ella and drove in a little bunch of cows, among them the three newly calved. One of them, a horned brindle heifer, showed the marks of some milking breed, but she was wild as a snake. She circled around, testing the spaces between the corral rails for a path to escape.

"Can I borrow her?" I said. "I'll bring her back with a fat calf at her side."

Out the window ...

We stampeded her up the loading chute and into my pickup. Arriving home, I backed tightly against the barn door and herded her down the narrow alley leading to the box stall where we milked. She charged into the stall, whirled around once or twice, and leaped out through the small 23" X 26" unbarred window, leaving the calf behind. We last saw her shouldering her way through the brush, climbing the mountain to higher ground.

"Oh this is a fine mess!" I scolded myself. "Now we have no milk, we have a calf to take care of, and maybe I'll have to pay for a cow." Discouraged, I started my pickup and headed up the rough farm road in the direction she had taken. I found her in a clearing on our flat top land. She threw up her head, defiant, then trotted off and at some distance, went back to grazing. I was powerless. On the open plains a rider on a good horse can overpower a cow and put her in a corral, but here no horse could help me. In this wooded country, with its brush and its greenbriers, I couldn't force that cow anywhere.

But we did hold the ace in the hole—we had her calf. I drove back to the house and hoped for the best.

Next morning the brindle cow was nosing around the barn with a full bag, calling softly to her calf. I closed the calf tightly in a separate stall, opened the barn door, and stood back. She walked in and I slammed the door shut behind her. She was in that same box stall—we had nailed slats over the window—and she spun around, trapped. Maeve called her, with her attitude and pointed horns, "intimidating."

My Mexican friends say, "El hambre es la mejor salsa," or "Hunger is the best sauce." I dished out a good measure of that seductive "sweet feed" into the feed box, and while she was eating I managed to close the homemade wooden stanchion on her neck. She fought like crazy but the stanchion held.

In my earlier days in Minnesota, when we had a cow that was bad to kick during milking, we often used "kickers," a

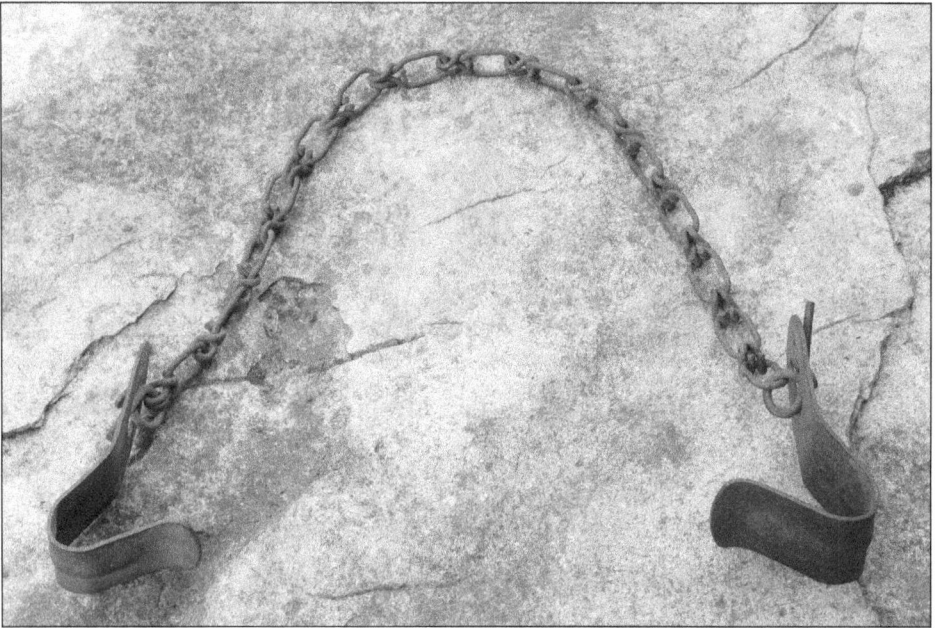

Kickers

PHOTO: CALEB COURTEAU

short adjustable chain with a U-shaped holder at each end that fitted around the large tendons just above the hocks to restrict violent movement. They worked fairly well—but I didn't have a pair.

I had something better, though. During my long years of breaking horses I had often used, as standard equipment, the Figure-8 hobble, to draw a colt's front legs closely together to prepare him for mounting (not to be confused with the Figure-8 hitch, used in halter-breaking). So for the brindle cow I took a light bundle of baling twine (a length of cotton rope, one half inch by about four feet, would have been better, but I didn't have one handy), I folded the ends around the cow's opposite hind leg (the left one), then took two twists between the legs and tied the ends together around the nearer right hind leg, forming a complete figure eight. I could now draw the legs tightly together. For supper that night our kids drank fresh cow's milk.

We fell into a routine. We kept the calf in the barn and fed it hay and calf manna and fresh water of course. Mornings and evenings, we would let the cow in for her sweet feed. We would milk from the cow what we needed and turn the calf in to suck out the rest. The cow grew gentle and I quit using the hobble.

Eventually we got our own milk cow and I hauled the brindle heifer back to Alvin's corral, with a healthy, chubby

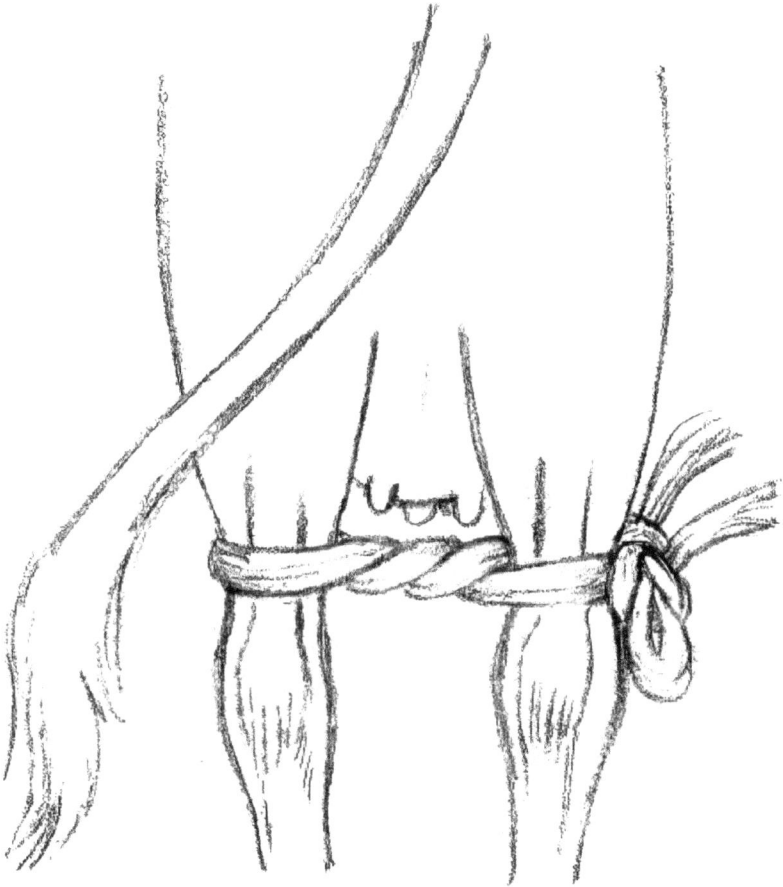

Pulling the cow's hind legs together with the Figure-8 hobble.

The milk cow she truly had become ...

calf at her side. I don't know what Alvin did with her, but he was an active trader with a way of getting things placed where they belonged, so it's quite likely she wound up in somebody's barn as the family milk cow she truly had become.

First published in Rural Heritage *December 2021/January 2022, pp. 46–47.*

Out of the Mouths of Rubes

The several branches of the family were gathered at a modest home atop Pinnacle Mountain here in hillbilly Madison County, Arkansas. The ostentatiously churchy matriarch of the clan was loudly proclaiming, "I know there's a heaven 'cause I seen it with my own eyes." Her son-in-law quietly grumbled aside, "I hope she took a good look around, 'cause it's the last time she'll ever get to see it." The amused kinsman who passed this story along added: "True, he was measuring her corn in his basket."

Country talk, my friends. The simple words of the simple folk.

Country folks seem always to have spoken in a figurative way, and most of their figures of speech come right out of a life with animals on the land. In an urban age, much of this colorful speech is fading. Back there in Washington, D.C., where my daughter Sarah wound up for awhile, folks found it quaint and amusing when she would use expressions like "a coon's age" or "three shakes of a lamb's tail," or "till the cows come home."

Much of this language is nothing short of poetic, if by poetry we mean something said in a indirect, roundabout, suggestive way that is more expressive than if it were stated in direct prose. Sarah, again, back in Washington, stopped along the highway to help a woman who had run out of gasoline. "They begged me to fill up," she said, "but I wouldn't listen. 'A hard head makes a soft biscuit.'" This delicate African-American adaptation of the somewhat

more vulgarly phrased Southern expression, "A hard head makes a soft ass [a spanked behind]," admonished to children, clearly implies that stubbornness begets contrary results.

Carl Vanlandingham had pulled my pickup out of a mud slick. I thanked him effusively. He dismissed my effusions, saying only, "It's a mighty long road that knows no bend." In other words, it would be a very long time, indeed, if he didn't need my help some day.

"A coon's age?"

I have always been fascinated by words and stories and clever language. Long before two serious accidents with horses, in quick succession, had crippled me up for a long period and led me into university studies and a brief teaching career, I had palavered in the jargon of my fellow cowboys. The average cowboy almost refuses to call a spade a spade if he can think of anything else to call it. His too-garrulous buddy or boss has "a bad case of the leaky mouth." That ranch hand he has to work with, who doesn't know how to properly align, set, and tamp a fencepost, is not dumb. He's just "a little weak north of the ears."

A cowboy never gets bucked off. He gets "ironed out" or gets his "head jabbed in the dirt." For that most dramatic of experiences, having a horse explode beneath you in a violent bucking fit, there are many descriptions: He "blew up," "blew the plug," "come uncorked," "come unwound," "grabbed hisself," or "turned the crank." The most descriptive of this fearsome event is, "He swallowed his tail," for the horse's head actually disappears between its front legs and its back arches upward in a crescent, leaving you "settin' on nothin' up there in the sky."

Having roped a steer by the horns, a roper might tell you, "I stacked my grass [his hemp rope] on his antlers." A favorite tactic of this verbal sport, everywhere in the rurals, is the saucy comeback: "Take it easy, Joaquín," I said to a top-notch rodeo clown. "If I don't, I'll have it done," he replied.

This kind of absurdity has always been a staple of country humor, and it's not just cowboys and Westerners talking. Back in my native Minnesota, a land of recent immigrants, still struggling with the new language and less articulate, a German, Norwegian, or Polish boy might have said, after a hard winter, "That cow is so thin she'd have to stand twice to cast a shadow."

The summer weather in Arkansas, at least here in the northwestern part, is famously erratic and unpredictable. The rains can be very local. You can watch the downpour across the hollow on your neighbor's pastures while your own garden and pastures remain parched. Natives—the locals that is—are fond of repeating, "You can set a double-barreled shotgun on its butt and it'll fill one barrel and leave the other bone-dry."

Earl Hankins, a farmer down on Fritts Creek, was known for his wit. A circle of neighbors were standing around visiting when the talk turned to the unpredictable weather. "About the only way I can tell if it's going to rain," pronounced one of the party, "is if it's thunderin' and lightnin' all around and pourin' rain straight down in the middle." Earl slapped his thigh and burst out, "Yep, and I've seen that fail too!"

Are country people inclined to speak more "poetically?" Can it be that there is more natural variety, drama, and excitement in their daily lives? However it be, country wit and country humor have their own distinctive flavor.

Much of this country-speak is regional or even local, related to custom and circumstance. Northwest Arkansas and the Ozarks in general are notorious for their plague of ticks. One wag posed the question, "Is it okay to pick ticks off in public?" The answer: "Sure, as long as they're your own ticks."

When I arrived in Arkansas in 1967, I discovered a language I hadn't known before. A "breachy" cow would go through fences, and a "rogue" bull would go anywhere. "Mast" was the nuts, mostly acorns, on which the hogs had till lately foraged and fattened. Arkansas had but recently passed a range law, requiring

"Yep, and I've seen that fail too!"

the enclosure of livestock, and folks were still calling unfenced land "the commons."

"Neighboring" has always been important to rural folks. When I started to leave after my first visit to my new Arkansas neighbors, they insisted, "You needn't rush off." Since we had already spent the entire evening visiting, that made me feel pretty welcome, but an even warmer expression of hospitality that I often heard later was, "Y'all hurry back now." The guest, on the other hand, might reply, "Better go home with me now," and I was to learn, from an elderly neighbor, that that could be an authentic invitation, for in the old, unhurried days before the automobile (which didn't arrive back here into the hills until the 1940s and '50s) and TV, and commercial entertainments, when folks mostly walked to their visits, the hosts would actually get up and stroll along toward the home of their guests to prolong the visit. "The work will always be there," I've so often heard, "you just have to take time to visit."

But visits can get too long, and the common expression, after an embarrassed look at the clock was, "Ma (or Pa), we'd better get up and go home so these folks can go to bed." If we can believe neighborhood gossip, one local patriarch, after yet another drowsy look at the clock, gave these words an ironic twist, saying, "Ma, we'd better get up and go to bed so these folks can go home."

I have dwelt a little here on the ways and words of Arkansas, my home now for more than 50 years, but I don't just write about Arkansawyers nor Westerners, nor cowboys nor farmers nor any group in particular. I write about, to, and for my own people, country people everywhere. Sure there are certain differences between different people from different parts, but wherever folks work with their hands and live close to the basics, I have found the same self-sufficiency, the same readiness to help each other out, and the same strong sense of cussed independence. I heard the following story some 70 years ago out in Montana. It was told as an honest-to-God truth, as something that had sure-nuff happened. Who knows? It maybe happened, or it could have happened, and certainly it should have happened. Certainly it could have happened here in Arkansas or anywhere else I have lived and worked on the farms and ranches of this nation.

Anyway, it seems this wealthy businessman from back East was the new owner of a big ranch, and he called in his foreman for instructions. "Now Jack," he said, "I'm a very busy man, and I'm a man of few words, so when you hear me whistle and look up here, you'll know I want you to drop everything and come a-runnin.'"

"Well sir," the foreman replied, "I, too, am a very busy man, and I, too, am a man of few words, so when you whistle up here and see me shakin' my head down there, you'll know damn well I ain't a-comin.'"

We all find our own line in the sand somewhere, but that kind of independence comes a lot harder when you're trying to hold onto what we in Arkansas call a "public job."

Sometimes it's hard to know whether what you're hearing is a stock expression, like a worn-out joke, or something fresh and individual, an original word or phrase. When I first came to Arkansas and phoned a new acquaintance with, "Is this Tom?" and Tom replied, "What's left of him," and later when I asked another friend, "How are you, Clyde?" and he answered, "No better," I thought these were pretty saucy comebacks, but I was soon to learn that locally, these were threadbare attempts at what once was thought to be wit. On the other hand, when Bob Hankins, farmer and roper, showed me the drayman's hitch for binding down a load of hay and finished the lesson with, "Now that's handy as a third hand," I thought I was hearing a timeworn figure of speech. I thought likewise when he later spoke of a neighbor as "odd as a three-dollar bill," but neither in the many, many years before nor since have I heard either of these expressions repeated, so might they possibly have been originals?

Sometimes just exaggeration is enough to get the idea across with vigor. Fred Baughman lived down the mountain with his quite large family. His rough tract was adjacent to our land, but from house to house by automobile it was five miles of extremely rough, steep, dirt road. "Fred," I urged, "why don't you come visit?"

"I'd like to visit, Dick," he said, "but with this crew of mine and that road that would be just about like moving."

Willie Gardner lived in the other direction, on a small farm so steep you could hardly stand up. He had no job other than that farm, yet his family was well fed, well clothed, and warm, and he drove a pretty good old pickup. "Willie Gardner could make a living on a flat rock," one neighbor remarked.

The utterances of Carl Vanlandingham, whom I have often quoted, sometimes had the force of maxim. All stockmen know the importance of keeping handy a sharp pocket knife. "I'd as soon be caught without my pants as caught without my knife," Carl once said. Or he could be metaphorical. Referring to the grueling demands of life back in the Ozark hills, he observed that "You've got to be a little lop-sided to live back here."

Carl enjoyed that vein of absurdity that runs through rural humor. Back in the '70s and '80s, when the population spillover from the cities began washing back into the hills, Carl complained, "If all these new folks don't quit comin' in, I'm going to move so far away I'll have to keep my own tomcat."

Country people have heard of sex, too, and they have plenty of humor on the topic, but really there is nothing rural or city or American or Mexican or Chinese about this topic. Interest in sex is universal. I relate the following tales only because these were the words of wisdom passed down by a couple of older men of the country.

Durf Drain was a World War II veteran, not terribly old but, in my mid-30s, much older than I. He was a small cattle farmer,

of the hard twist, Levis-wearing, roll-your-own-Bull-Durham kind. We had developed an easy friendship. As he leaned against the big wheel of my dump rake one day, visiting while my team rested, I asked him, half in jest and half curious, "Hey, Durf, how's that love life work at your age?"

"Well I'll tell ya," he said, "It gets richer. It takes a lot less to do ya."

Back in the '80s, I put in about three years working on the roads of Lincoln County, Nebraska. One of the three commissioners who supervised the road work of this huge county was an older gentleman, nearing retirement. He was a good boss, well-liked by his men, with whom he had a friendly and familiar—but respectful—relationship, often kidding around. "Hey Chief," one of the boys joked one day, "how's them bedroom chores going for ya?"

"Bedroom chores?" the "chief" said. "You'd never believe how far behind you can get and how fast you can get caught up!"

A self-deprecating thread runs through much of country humor. Alvin Diehl (about 1910 to the mid 1990s) was a cowboy of the old-time kind, working as a young man on the big outfits of West Texas. Approaching middle age, he wanted his own place, and the only affordable land left was in places like the hills of Arkansas. He bought a farm on High Rock Mountain, five miles beyond our Pinnacle Mountain ranch. By hard work and dogged, skillful trading, he eventually expanded and developed it into one of the few bona fide cattle ranches in this part of the county, but the first few years were hard. To earn a living, he just milked a few cows, and then they shut the milk route down.

During those lean years, Alvin and Mrs. Diehl had visitors from back home. As they were leaving, Alvin quipped, "Tell all my friends back in Texas that I'm still wearing a Stetson hat—but don't tell them it's the same one I was wearing when I left."

"Oh Arkansas!" I have often lamented of this hard land, "Arkansas, graveyard of dreams!"

The following is told as frankly a joke, but one with a realistic edge: Again a Texan, returning to his native land, announced with a boast: "No sir, them Arkies didn't get to me. I didn't have but $150,000 when I went there, and I come back with a good ol' Chevy pickup and three of the best coon dogs in the state."

Finally, we have some stories that are just plain jokes with a rural twist. I heard this one at a sale barn: A cattle farmer from the hill country boards the plane at our big Northwest Arkansas airport and takes his seat. He's dressed in worn Levis, a snap-button shirt, scuffed Western boots, and a narrow-brimmed hat with a greasy hatband. A tall, broad-shouldered gentleman, in a pressed frontier suit with a lustrous broad-brimmed Stetson hat and alligator boots, comes down the aisle and takes his seat by the Arkansawyer. The extroverted Texan looks at his seat-mate and perceives they might have something in common, so he strikes up a conversation.

"You look like you might be a stockman," he says.

"I run about 50 mother-cows," the Arkie replies. "How about you, you run a few cows?"

"I calve out between nine and ten thousand head and winter over several hundred steers. You have some kind of crew for your little operation?"

"Oh," modestly answers the Arkansas man, "mostly just me and the wife. Sometimes we hire a couple of high school kids at haying time or to help with fencin.' How about you?"

"I keep a dozen cowboys hired full-time, and five or six men on maintenance and keepin' the fences up."

They sit in silence, 'til the Texan asks, "Well now, how much land you need to run them 50 cows?"

"I own 320 acres," the other man replies, "but it ain't all fenced. Lots of rocks and bluffs and scrub oak. Land that ain't fit for nothin' but to hold the earth together. What's it take to run your big herd?"

"Let me put it this way—when I get in my pickup in the morning and head out, I still haven't reached my western line by sundown."

"I know just what you're talkin' about!" exclaims the Arkansas man. "I used to have an old truck like that myself."

The following story I heard as a joke, but I swear it must have actually happened up there in the Minnesota of my childhood and youth. Several farm magazines were then offered in print, like *The Farm Journal, The Country Gentleman,* and others. Young men would chug through the countryside in their old automobiles, trying to sell subscriptions to make a little money. The story was always that the young salesman was trying to work his way through college. One such young man spotted a farmer plowing and hoofed it across the turned furrows to where the farmer stopped his tractor to greet this visitor. The boy immediately went into his spiel: "On page 17," he said, "there's an article on the weaning weights of calves of the different beef breeds, and on page 35 there's an article on the need to balance corn for hogs with a little animal protein, and here on page 48 there's a comparison of the nutrient contents of the different grains, and here's an advertisement for a new eight-way wrench, and here ..."

The farmer listened patiently and politely with his old John Deere two-lunger put-put-bang-banging away at an idle. Finally, he interrupted and said, "Son, I don't want to offend you or hurt your feelings. I know you've got a good product there and I could probably learn a lot, but hell, son, I ain't farmin' half as well as I know how to now."

I don't know anyone, anywhere, in any walk of life, who couldn't identify.

First published in Rural Heritage *June/July 2022, pp. 38–43.*

Country Justice Part 1:

Country Justice from the Bench

Author's note: Normally I write, in Rural Heritage, *mostly about animals and our involvement with them, the theme most central to our shared rural experience, but today I write of our culture. Yes, we do have a rural culture. By "culture" I do not mean lace tablecloths, high-toned musical tastes, and impeccable grammar. I mean our humor, our figures of speech and our ways and customs, which may not be totally different from those of the big city but do have their own distinctive flavor. "Country" is just a little bit different.*

Madison County is one of the most rural in Arkansas, maybe in the nation. Until a few years ago, we didn't have a single traffic light. Now we still have only one in the county.

One of the ways in which I believe our old rural society was different is that it was easier to be young. Men and boys, women and girls worked shoulder to shoulder in close company, so there was less distance between the generations, and the foibles of teenagers or twenty-somethings could be more easily tolerated or negotiated. I have no hard evidence to support this opinion, just the observations and reflections of an old man who has seen a lot of life in the boondocks.

Here, I'll share two different stories of justice, one of justice dispensed and another of justice received, in rural America.

* * * * *

"You're a one-armed bandit!" the defendant reportedly taunted the judge. A bandit he was not, but Judge WQ Hall, judge of the district court at Huntsville, Madison County, Arkansas, was certainly one-armed, and with the stub of his other arm fastened to a prosthetic hook, and with his Ford Thunderbird parked outside and his breezy, informal manner in court, almost bantering at times, he was the most colorful public figure I have ever witnessed in action—and in my opinion, he was in the right place and doing the right thing. But in the summer of 2003, he found himself not judging but being judged.

It came about like this. Jack Gates, an older man who owned a small waste disposal business, had been videotaped dumping human waste on a farmer's meadow and was brought before Judge Hall's court. The defendant pleaded guilty so there was no trial, only the sentencing, and at this point the reporting and the facts become unclear. Evidently, during the sentencing, a heated exchange took place, and the judge was subsequently accused of spitting on the defendant and calling him "scum" and a "liar" and threatening to kill him. He was accordingly called before a disciplinary commission to answer charges. WQ—close friends called him simply "Q"—responded of course in self-defense, and the most believable account to come of the inquiry was that Judge Hall had told the defendant that if he brought that stuff out to Madison County and dumped it on his land "he would be shot." That sounds to me like country-speak, the way a lot of folks talk out here. I don't believe many of us would take those words as a truly serious death threat.

Nevertheless, it would be, without question, unjudicial conduct, and WQ, pleading poor health and bad hearing, resigned as district judge and no further action was taken.

Thus he resigned under a cloud, so to honor his long and valuable service to the communities of our rural county, I felt moved to write the following letter, which appeared as a guest editorial in our local weekly on October 30, 2003.

"A Day in Court with Judge WQ Hall," guest editorial, *Madison County Record,* **Thursday, October 30, 2003.**

"I know but for the whims of fate you might be sitting here and I'd be standing there," he tells the defendant, then goes on to say that nevertheless, it's his job to judge and judge he must. That's WQ Hall's court—personal, flamboyant, but ever steeped in and guided by a deep respect for the law. Judge Hall has been much in the public eye recently, and it now seems my duty, to the man himself if not to my fellow citizens, to speak my mind.

Some years ago, I had occasion to sit through a session in Judge Hall's Court. I watched for a few minutes, then reached for pen and paper and began to jot down notes, for it was clear that I was witnessing a remarkable example of our judicial system in action. I'll report my observations and reflections as recorded that afternoon, in the present tense, unbiased by previous experience, personal acquaintance, or political affiliation.

Judge Hall is human. He is charged with rendering justice, but it's clear that that justice will be tempered by sympathy for human frailty, and that he knows his people well, often knows the individual himself and his or her family.

He questions at length a small young woman of 19 about her second DWI offense and remarks how bad her family must feel. He seems more interested in getting his mostly young defendants straightened out and staying out of future trouble than in meting out harsh punishment.

He is especially serious while talking to those arrested for drinking and driving. He sternly lectures one young man who had led an officer on a high-speed chase, telling him, "We'll read about you causing an officer to be killed or causing yourself to be killed, or causing someone else to be killed."

Recognizing our total dependence, in these rural areas, on the automobile, he is very reluctant to remove driving privileges completely. He tells more than one young defendant

One young man seems to evoke profound sympathy.

that "this Court" will not fine you for driving without a license while going to work, but we'll sure get you for driving to a pool hall, a dance, or the liquor store.

One young man seems to evoke profound sympathy. Judge Hall observes that the boy has been in jail a long time on his third DWI charge. He says he knows the boy is a very hard worker and has been the best trusty they've ever had at the jail. He remarks that the boy had been abandoned by his father, and he lectures him on the serious risk he runs of winding up in prison on a fourth DWI charge. He does not want to see him "go south," and he pleads with him, earnestly pleads, to stop drinking.

Judge Hall is a bit of an actor, and he seems to enjoy his stage, but he is also deeply aware of his role as an educator of the public, and that, above all, he is there to dispense justice— true justice, not just punishment.

Two young brothers are charged with possession of alcohol by a minor. The younger, a boy of about eighteen, pleads guilty along with his brother. WQ now adds to his role as judge that of legal counsel. He questions the boy further and then advises him that on the basis of what the boy has told him, he is not guilty, should not plead guilty, and wonders why he has done so. He then swivels his chair a little and addresses the audience.

"You've got to have the beer in your possession. It's not enough that they thought you were going to drink the beer, or even that the beer was on the seat and you intended to drink the beer at a later time. They, the arresting officers, have to prove that you were actually drinking the beer for this Court to find you guilty." He enters a "not guilty" plea and sets a court date.

He keeps up a folksy tone, and he draws defendants into a circle of intimacy, or at least confidence, with an occasional off-hand reference to his own failings, past and even present. "You boys," he says, "You're like the Hall boys. You like the taste of liquor." All the while, though, he's delivering the message that, though we're all weak and frail, there's the Law above us all to guide and counsel and control us, and I'm not judging you self-righteously as an individual, but as an instrument of that Law.

He puts on quite a show. There's even humor, though it's not all provided by WQ himself. It turns out that even a police report can contain a laugh or two. WQ reads: "Let's see. Officer X spotted you driving in an erratic manner south of Kingston. He chased you three miles at speeds up to 80 m.p.h. Says you were drinking whiskey from a peanut butter jar on the seat beside you. You said you thought the flashing blue light in your rearview mirror was a farmer's yardlight. A farmer's yardlight? That's not a very good defense."

It's an improvised show, and nobody can keep up that kind of an extemporaneous flow without making a few mistakes. The banter verges, at moments, almost upon buffoonery, and there are slips, faux pas, maybe an occasional lapse into what some might consider bad taste, but throughout it all, Judge Hall never lets his public forget that the law is a serious matter. He shows little sympathy for one young man who has received four tickets for speeding within a short period. This fellow has a good job, is a productive member of society, and Judge Hall, thinking out loud for his courtroom audience, in balancing the scales of justice, observes that the defendant has received no DWI citations and has had no accidents, and that this is in his favor, yet he is much troubled by the young man's apparently cavalier attitude toward the law. "What's the matter ... you just don't care whether you get a ticket?" he says. When the boy is making arrangements to pay his fine later because he's had to make a car payment and can't pay today, WQ scolds him sharply, saying, "You keep getting those tickets and can't pay them, you won't be needing a car. You'll be riding a mule."

So the afternoon is not without its harsher moments. One young man who comes before the Court is attending the University and drives a Porsche. He tries to counter the "rich-boy" image by reporting that he worked on a hog farm during the summer, but it turns out that his father owns the farm, and this brings him in for some derision. My wife has pointed out that being prosperous and driving a fancy car is no crime, and maybe the kid did work hard on his father's farm, so maybe he deserved the same gentler approach as the errant mill hands, loggers, or whatever.

It's a valid point, and it could be that WQ is a little too populist in his predispositions, but I can honestly say that, except perhaps for a certain tone, the scales of justice were not weighted that afternoon, one ounce this way or that, between individuals. I earnestly hope that I, myself, might never be summoned before the law to answer for any of the offenses judged that afternoon, but "it's a mighty long road that knows no bend," so even if that comes to pass, may the court that judges me be as measured and even-handed as the court I watched presided over by a certain Judge WQ Hall out here in the "boonies" of Madison County, Arkansas.

—Dick Courteau, Pinnacle Community

POSTSCRIPT

WQ Hall was killed, as a passenger, in a one-car crash, in 2017, at age 88. A lot of us felt pretty bad.

First published in Rural Heritage *August/September 2022, pp. 22–24.*

Country Justice Part 2:

Country Justice at the Other End

Ihave written of justice dispensed, with mercy and wisdom, by an avuncular judge in the heart of the hillbilly country of Arkansas. Now let me jump 1,200 miles to the northwest, and backwards a little in time, to tell of the rather paternal justice received in another country setting. I tell this story mainly to point out how times have changed for our young people between the very rural then of my day and the more urban-oriented now of these times.

Only once, in the rough-and-tumble life of my youth, did I get myself thrown into jail. In the spring of 1954, during a very eventful few weeks for me, I had won money at the Hot Springs, Montana, rodeo within the Flathead Indian Reservation. Since placing among the top riders was always cause for celebration, I celebrated—big time! Starting with a few beers at the Silver Dollar, I then went to the town's café, along with my new friend Zack X, for a hamburger dinner. Zack and I were served our meal where we sat in a booth.

And now for a little background: Whatever rank and standing we RCA cowboys held within our own organization, we were the proud pros and we were pretty disdainful of the general run of riders. Especially irritating to us was the all-too-occasional individual who boasted of the riding prowess of some uncle, cousin, or other kinsman, friend, or neighbor.

In the booth behind me, a young Indian man was loudly extolling the skills and feats of some one or another of his circle. I slowly pivoted in my booth and, not in a hostile tone but beer-mellow and a little sarcastically—and totally out of line—I commented that, "I bet he was a rank S.O.B."

My adversary—as he instantly became—leaped to his feet, furious, and began cursing and challenging me. Unbelievably, he jutted out his chin and kept shouting, "Just hang it on me! Go ahead, just take your best lick! Just hang it on me!" I staggered to my feet and stood facing him, befuddled by this sudden turn of events, when Zack X, returning from the restroom, came up behind me and growled, "Well hang it on the so-and-so." Bystanders later said that I turned and looked at Zack, slowly and almost thoughtfully, and replied, "Okay," then came up from the waist with a haymaker that struck that jutted-out jaw with such force that the guy went down and hit the floor so hard they thought he was out of action for the night. But this fellow was tough. He sprang to his feet and tackled me, but at that moment the owner of the café, a large and powerful man, burst from behind the counter and threw both of us out the door, one after the other. We landed in the curbside gutter and tangled again.

A sudden cloudburst, shortly before, had sent a strong stream of water rushing down that gutter. I have always been afraid of the water, and since I wasn't getting the best of this scuffle anyway, it was a relief when the town constable and his deputy-for-the-night threw us in an automobile and hauled us to the jail, a recently built homemade affair, where we were locked into adjacent cells. I was to spend there the most miserable night of my life.

And now let me digress in a brief aside: An amusing tale about this jail had already become town legend by that night of my incarceration. The little structure had been jerry-rigged into shape simply by welding together sheets of plate metal to form a couple of crude cells beneath a roof. The local welder hired to do the job, after leaving work one day when the structure was nearly completed, had gone on a bender and had gotten into a scrape with the law, so he'd wound up in the same jail he had just built and was left to cool it out. After sleeping several hours, he woke up and found he'd been locked into the very cell where he'd left his cutting torch. He fired up the torch, cut a big hole in the wall, and walked out to freedom. Evidently the entertainment value to the town was considered sufficient payment for his offense, for I never heard that any charges for jailbreaking had ever been pressed.

In the cell where I was deposited, the only facility of any kind was a one-person cot, on which lay an extremely obese man, evidently in an alcoholic stupor. The narrow strip of mattress not covered by my cellmate's bulk was inadequate to accommodate even my smallish frame. Our only covering was a thin sheet-blanket with a hole in it two feet wide, and that hole was on my side. With my adversary in that brawl earlier, I had gotten soaked in the gutter and though it was June, it was night in the mountains and as the chill grew deeper I shivered almost convulsively. Worst of all, I had drunk that beer, and the cell had no toilet facilities, so the discomfort of retention soon grew into pain and the pain into agony. (I was to learn later that the town could have been sued to the limit for holding locked prisoners unattended.)

Eventually the sky lightened and I and my erstwhile antagonist, in the adjoining cell, began commiserating about our bursting bladders. Curious about this fellow I had fought, I stooped to peer through one of the small round holes in the panels of metal plate. What I saw was—another eyeball! We both burst out laughing.

About mid-morning the constable came to release us. After instantaneously seeking bodily relief, my foe and I walked companionably up to Main Street and parted. The constable had instructed me, word of mouth only, to appear before the justice of the peace. Three days later, this elderly gentleman returned from a trip somewhere. He had received no notice whatever of the case, knew not a single detail, so I had to explain, in honorable objectivity, what the town's charges against me might be, and then to offer explanations in defense of my actions that evening so as to request leniency. I had therefore, in a sense, to serve as both my own prosecution and my own defense.

The justice thought a few moments, then asked, "How about a fine of $10? Does that seem reasonable to you?" It did. I paid and the case was closed. (Remember, $10 then meant about $100 now.)

I believe that in today's more urban-oriented society, the law would be harder on a young person committing an infraction like mine. (Incidentally, I haven't even mentioned that I was still a little underage for drinking.) The court setting would be less personal and the youth would not be likely to come before a Solomonic judge like W.Q. Hall, who might even counsel him in his defense, nor would he be likely to be judged by a grandfatherly old justice who would reason out a penalty which seemed fair to both defendant and the rule of law.

The fine would probably be heavier and if a vehicle were involved and there had been drinking, an "interlock" would be ordered for the accused's vehicle to keep it from moving unless the driver could blow an alcohol-free breath. The interlock is an effective deterrent and its use in sentencing is eminently logical and just, but the "criminal" has to pay for the installation and then keep paying monthly to have it serviced. If their old vehicle goes belly up and they have to buy another, they'll have to pay for the transfer and re-installation of the device. All this paying and paying can be especially hard if the guilty one has trouble finding or keeping their job, which could happen if the violation involved certain drug offenses, and drugs are everywhere now to trip up the young. Every offense seems to go on record, and oh, how those records keep following the offender! A serious blot can impair job opportunities or block chances for financial aid in education. Youthful error can thus too easily cascade into prolonged misfortune. I know something of these matters. My wife Maeve and I have had four high-spirited sons.

I have no hard data to support the following opinion, only the experience of a very long life lived mostly in the country, and that experience leaves me with the impression—the certainty, almost—that it was easier to grow up in those old rural places than in today's more urban-slanted society. It is true, probably, that my generation worked harder physically, but our path forward was more clearly marked and we had fewer stumbling blocks in our way. An errant past was more quickly forgotten or forgiven, and the young were more easily given a second chance. In my own case, back there waiting for my life to take hold, the world gave me chance after chance after another second chance. That ten-dollar fine in Montana was not the last of them.

First published in Rural Heritage *August/September 2022, pp. 26–28.*

Our Auctioneers: Poets, Salesmen, and Philosophers

The big team—Percherons, as I recall—were driven into the ring and a lively bidding struck right up. The team were well-matched and of cookie-cutter conformation. They appeared very calm, though young, and they handled well, ground driven. The bidding went quickly upward and when it slowed, the auctioneer dropped the increments to $50 and began to work the crowd. "They're a nice pair of young horses just coming into their own," he declared. "You can buy this pair, work 'em a couple of years, and they'll make money for you every day you've owned them." The bidding started up again slowly, but the price was way up there now and the action soon came to a halt. The auctioneer paused in his chant, lowered the increment to $25, and—looking earnestly at potential buyers, advised—"I tell ya what, boys, supper will taste a lot better tonight if you buy them than it will if you don't."

There you have it, folks, a country auction and a country auctioneer—marketing, entertainment, and barnyard psychology, all rolled into one.

The first auction I ever attended, at the age of eight, was in March, 1941. Auctions were traditionally held in early spring in those northern states (Minnesota in this case), when the harsh winter was about over and planting was yet to begin, and a family could still move to another rented farm or to some

*"Supper will taste
a lot better tonight
if you buy them than
it will if you don't."*

other work. At this particular auction, a pathetically incapable family were selling their few thin cows and their woe-be-gone team and a few other meager possessions and were moving to Minneapolis, where they might do better at a factory job.

Auctions have always been a big part of rural life. The weekly livestock auctions, the farm auctions, the horse auctions, even a land auction once in awhile. The regular commercial livestock auctions, essential as they are to our farm economy, are not nearly as interesting as the farm and horse actions. These commercial livestock auctions are "cried" by professionals who have attended specialists' schools to be trained in that stylized chant so difficult for many of us laypeople to follow. They address themselves mostly to a few professional buyers sitting in a front row who respond in ways almost imperceptible to the onlooker, like a slight nod or the flick of a card. The lots being sold, of cattle let's say, are uniform in class, size, and color. The bidding is almost mechanical.

Farm and horse auctions were, and are, more colorful and varied. At the farm auctions, anything might be sold. Starting with the household items, the auctioneers worked their way toward the larger stuff outside. Along the way, for a pittance, you might buy a grab-bag box or bucket full of nuts and bolts or some other miscellaneous assortment of odds and ends. Finally, the really large items would sell: tractors and farm machinery; cars or trucks; livestock; sometimes the farm itself.

These farm auctions doubled as social occasions, where friends and neighbors bumped into each other and visited. There was coffee and lunch, occasionally free, always reasonable.

I haven't seen, for quite a few years now, any of those large colored handbills announcing a farm sale and advertising the offerings, that used to be left for pickup in local cafés, gas stations, bars, etc., nor have I seen, along our country roads, those quarter-mile-long lines of cars and pickups, with a crowd in the farmyard, that used to indicate that an auction was being held. Is another rural tradition slipping away?

Anyway, it's the horse auctions that have always been of most interest to me, for that's where my life has been—among the horses. Horse auctions are more interesting to me than horse shows. At the auctions you see more variety and uncertainty, and you sense the pull of the potential. One sees the different breeds and kinds of horses, and the different sizes, ages, and colors. Different levels of training are often on display. And it's here at the horse auctions that the most entertaining auctioneers ply their trade, with wit and clever words, trying, directly and more personally, ever to draw another bid from the crowd.

They have to keep that smooth flow of chanting palaver going. It's all about that sing-song flow of words, though sometimes the auctioneer will pause dramatically, directly addressing the individual, trying to coax another bid from an uncertain buyer.

To keep that flow going, an auctioneer must fall back at times on what seems to be a reservoir of stock expressions. Like when an ordinary mare was ridden into the ring at Harrison, Arkansas. She was walked and trotted around the ring a little and she neck-reined but only just so-so. Auctioneer Rodney calls out, "She's got ride in her hide!" Later, the bidding was going low on a nondescript two-year-old and Rodney shouts, "He's cheaper 'n a new broom!"

It was at one of the Missouri sales that the auctioneer shouted, "They're the right kind, the right age, and they're right here," thereby calling attention, in that one swift, rhythmical declaration, to the qualities of the team while at the same time slipping in the suggestion that there's no need to drive maybe hundreds of miles more, folks—what you've been looking for is "right here!"

It was up at Hillsboro, North Dakota, at the age of 15, that I heard the first of these catchy phrases. The year was 1948, post WWII, when American farmers and the nation had been rushing into mechanization with an unquestioning zeal that was almost religious. (More than one farmer had commented, with approval it seemed, that "Soon you'll have to go to a zoo to see a horse.") Thousands upon thousands of horses were being dumped on the market, to be sold for slaughter at prices that seem today almost free. Among them were thousands of good work horses with names like Sally and Nelly, Rex and King, that had for years been earning their keep in the fields growing food for Americans and the world.

At Hillsboro that day, a large team of gray mules were driven in, tall and rangy with their long ears and deep-set sorrowful eyes. Their gray was so bleached out by the years you could call it white. Mules were not common in that northern state, and the auctioneer, to highlight the novelty, looked at them slowly, then reflected aloud, "The load is never too heavy and the road is never too long."

Coming back closer in time, Maeve and I were up at the big Columbia, Missouri, drafthorse sale when a snappy, smart-looking colt comes trotting in. The bidding picks right up and the auctioneer, keeping things upbeat and lively, cries out, "You came to buy one, buy a good one!"

Back again in Harrison, Arkansas, a Fox Trotter mare comes pounding into the ring in an elegant showing-off of her gait and action. Though high-strung and energetic, the rider quickly settles her into a flat walk and then further calms her to stand quietly. Rodney boasts, "Just like electricity, you can turn it on when you need it and turn it off when you don't."

At another sale, a mare is shown in hand, not ridden or hitched. The owner explains that she is nervous to hitch but once hitched is a safe worker and a good puller. Any declaration of a flaw in temperament is bound to depress the price, so as the bidding limps along, the auctioneer points out, "She's not very high, there'll be no gamble here."

A good auctioneer knows which angle to come from. Of course, it's the many uses of the horse that attract and hold us horse people. We handle cattle on horseback and horses pull our wagons and plows and carry our bodies from A to B. The auctioneer will talk to those points as appropriate. It's the unique beauty of the horse, though, that adds so much extra appeal and turns a lot of us otherwise practical-minded folks into ardent devotees. Auctioneers play to this, our weakness. A very flashy team of black-and-white mares was selling over in Oklahoma. The bidding had gone maybe as far as it was going to go, but the auctioneer, working the crowd for one last bid, shouted, "They would bring that if they were any color, but look at that color! You boys are all on the right track but only one of you will take them home." Notice, besides the appeal to the buyers' sense of beauty, the subtle prod given to their sense of competition—"only one of you...."

At the big Columbia sale, an exceptionally beautiful team was on the block. "You may not work 'em every day," the auctioneer loudly pointed out, "but you'll be lookin' at 'em every day!" It's a thought.

Sometimes an animal is brought through the ring that doesn't represent the species at its most beautiful best. The auctioneer is ready. Like, again, up at that Columbia sale, when two or three teams had come down from bitter cold Minnesota. The first team came in looking shaggy in their rough winter coats. The bidding got under way but was unenthusiastic. The auctioneer jumped in, questioning loudly, "Has anybody took a look? They're in their everyday clothes. It's been 25 below where they come from." When the bidding failed to pick up, he scolded, "I tell ya what, you're wrong here." On another of the Minnesota teams, the auctioneer apologizes, "I know they got a lot of hair, but they need that where they come from."

When the bidding is low, we hear implicit warnings that a bargain might be slipping away. "You're wrong here!" the auctioneer insists, or he questions, puzzled, "You gonna let me do that, boys?" Exasperated, he chides, "This is the worst thing we've done all day!"

I think that the highest demand placed upon an auctioneer's persuasive talents is when he must find the upper reaches of the monetary value of a high-dollar animal. Many years ago, a well-known horse trader down in Texas was asked, "What's a horse worth these days?" He replied, "An old $65 horse is worth about $65, but a good horse is worth whatever you can get for him." An auctioneer's job is to reach for the sky.

The bidding is still low on an attractive young horse and doesn't seem to be going much higher. The auctioneer cries, "There ain't a man in this world knows what that colt is worth but it sure wouldn't cost much to find out, a little later on."

Another auctioneer lectures: "You spend your money any way you want, but I tell ya what, $100 means nothing on a mare like that." And as an old horseman myself, I can personally assure the reader that the man spoke truth. One hundred dollars should mean nothing, measured against future feed bills, pleasure and usefulness, and possible safety issues, whether that sum was back in my day or during these modern times.

It was an auctioneer down at London, Arkansas, who most neatly put his finger on this problem of "How much?" The bidding had risen to more than $2,000, a very high figure for that time and place. The auctioneer, unwilling to let the action stop, had reduced the increments to $25, and he reasoned with the few buyers still hanging on. "Who can tell," he mused, "within $25 what a horse like this is worth?" His argument was solid. Had I been there to buy a horse, and this was the right one, why and when would I have stopped short of another 25 dollars? Logically, only when I didn't have 25 dollars left.

Not all my stories come from high-powered auctioneers at major auctions. Steve Nichols, very young at the time, served as one of the auctioneers who spelled each other at Chester Palmer's mid-sized annual horse sale over in Afton, Oklahoma. Steve had no college degree, that I know of, nor do I believe he had graduated from auctioneer's school, but he had been known in high school as a witty kid with the gift of gab.

As an adjunct to the Afton sale, spaces were rented along the walls of the large Quonset hut that served as the sale pavilion to vendors who sold small farm items, even household items. In a mop-up operation, Steve was auctioning off the unsold leftovers from these "booths." Two pitchforks came up, of the old wooden-handled kind. I won the bid. Steve offered me both. I chose one. "Man has only one horse," Steve rattled off matter-of-factly. There was nothing especially remarkable about the comment except that Steve wove this little absurdity into his chattering chant without a break in stride.

Immediately a few housewares were offered, among them a pair of rolling pins. They sold for one quick dollar. "There ya go," Steve quipped, "two pins for one dough!"

"Two pins for one dough!"

I have woven into the narrative above an ample sampling of the phrasings and figures of speech, the appeals and admonitions, that our auctioneers employ to persuade folks to spend their money. I am sure my readers could add many more, but these are a representative sampling of a day at the auction. Incidentally, by way of full disclosure, I may have become occasionally mixed up as to the precise details, but every line enclosed within quotation marks is, word for word, something I heard and recorded in the little notebook I have customarily carried at my side. All, that is, except those quoted from my teen years.

It was at the sale in Billings, Montana. I was about 17. A tough-looking cowboy rode into the ring—but wait! First, I must lay a little background.

Horse people should be guided by a code of ethics, as should we all. "Honor thy word and do not conceal the truth," should be the horseperson's first commandment. If an individual selling a horse thinks their animal is over at the knees, or is too low in the withers, or too stubby in the pasterns, they are perfectly entitled to keep that opinion to themselves, but if the animal bucks, kicks, runs away, or stumbles dangerously, it is a grave wrong not to disclose this vice. The Bible itself underpins this view:

> If a bull gores a man or woman to death, the bull is to be stoned to death, and its meat must not be eaten. But the owner of the bull will not be held responsible. If, however, the bull has had the habit of goring and the owner has been warned but has not kept it penned up and it kills a man or woman, the bull is to be stoned and its owner also is to be put to death. However, if payment is demanded, the owner may redeem his life by the payment of whatever is demanded.
> New International Version, 21 Exodus 28:30

Forty-some years ago, I drove 300 miles to deal for a five-year-old Thoroughbred mare, reportedly green broke. The mare was led from her stall, and without a word of counsel or caution, I mounted. She was high-strung and green as a gourd but she was kitten-gentle and carried me around with absolute unconcern. I trailered her home and rode her daily. After three weeks, she blew up one day without warning into a frantic bucking fit. Talking later to her former owner, this lady blurted out, "Why that mare can buck harder than anything I've ever seen!"

I have often, through the years, puzzled over that lady and her failure to forewarn me that day. Did she think that to an old bronc rider, which she knew I had been, bucking doesn't really matter? (It matters!) Was she so anxious to get the mare sold out of her stable that she slipped into denial, telling herself something like ... "Oh well, she doesn't always buck, maybe she won't buck this time"? Whatever the reason or reasons, regarding the seriousness of mounting an unsuspecting rider on an unpredictable horse, this lady just didn't "get it." And she couldn't have known that during those three weeks, I would carry one day my precious baby daughter on the back of that slowly ticking time-bomb.

Now, back to that cowboy at Billings, about 1950. He rode in on a snorty, wild-eyed colt, tense and all drawn up with just a little hump in its back. The colt hardly responded to the crude plow rein. He was barely green broke, not far from a raw bronc, and he wasn't being presented as anything other. From the bleachers a voice called out, "Can a kid ride him?" The cowboy turned in his saddle, looked at the father incredulously, pulled the cigarette from his lips, and called back, "If you got a right tough kid!"

That cowboy, he got it.

And now, a last word about horse auctions, and the folks that run them, as expressed by the old horse trader Johnny Watkins. All his life, Johnny has bought and sold all things country with the gift of a born trader, but his specialty has been, for a half-century at least, horses. Johnny is one of the more colorful, and certainly one of the most simpatico of the personages I have run across during this long life of gypsying through the barns and pastures, corrals and arenas of this nation. Speaking one day of the chicanery at horse sales, of the need that "buyer beware!" must always be kept uppermost in mind, Johnny summed it up this way: "If you buy a horse at an auction and you get him home and he ain't crippled or half blind or he don't buck you off, why, you done brought home the wrong horse!"

First published in Rural Heritage *October/November 2022, pp. 26–31.*

Irony at the Auction

The Counterfeit

Smoky was a counterfeit. At birth, he was the prettiest foal, of any breed, that had ever been dropped in my barn or on my pastures, and he wasn't really any breed at all. His dam was a large, 14-hand Haflinger mare, strongly built and square, a wonderful worker and puller in the harness and good transportation under the saddle, but the sire was unknown. We had purchased the mare as "open," not pregnant, but after three or four months she showed some belly, and in the fullness of time, she bagged up and foaled.

Smoky was jet black. He promised to be of ideal conformation for a small dual-purpose horse. Square-built and with good withers like his dam, he was a little more refined than she, with clean limbs and full strong hooves. His head was neat and broad between the eyes. He was a beauty.

Smoky had gentle in his blood, at least on his dam's side, and growing up between her and me, in field and stall, he was a puppy dog. The winter he was coming three, I mounted him in a box stall many times. He remained unconcerned. I would bridle him with a snaffle bit and flex him left and right, and at the poll, preparing him for future training. Busy always, I did not get around to really start breaking him till he was three coming four. Beginning work in our round corral, when he was guiding lightly and travelling out well at the walk and trot, I took him out of the corral and into the pastures and along our dirt roads. Now the disillusionment began. Once outside his familiar everyday surroundings, Smoky was afraid of everything—a plastic bag, a boulder or bush, a shed along the road, a tractor parked in a field, cows across the fence. Strangely enough, like other horses I've known of similar disposition, he wasn't afraid of moving cars or trucks, things he should have been afraid of.

This irrational fear of things is more than a blemish in a horse you want to use—it's a serious fault. Some horses suddenly leap so explosively sideways it's almost impossible for even an accomplished rider to remain in the saddle. Smoky was not an extreme case. When he shied, he was not hard to ride, and he did not try to bolt. It's just that he was very, very suspicious, and when he was unsure of a thing, he would refuse to continue along the road or trail and try to turn back.

His fault was not really a danger to a good rider, it was more a continual irritation. Smoky was not fun to ride. To offset this bad habit, he had no particular redeeming virtue, like maybe a fast walk or a feather-light "handle," that might have justified my spending more time on him. I decided to sell him at public auction and let some other horseperson take him over. I was almost 80. I hoped to get $200 or $300 for him.

One thing about Smoky had improved as he matured—his looks! With his trim build, his arched neck, and proud bearing, he would have been an eye-catcher anywhere. Our Mexican neighbor, as I rode through her acres one day, pronounced him "presumido"—proudly vain. He had turned an iron gray, and his finest point of pride was his lustrous coat with the abundant mane and tail, luxuriant as that of a draft horse. Gently pulling a few hairs here and there, I trimmed the mane to a uniform shape and did the same with the tail, leaving it broad and a little long. We gathered his tack and trailered him up to the sale at Diamond, Missouri.

We were assigned a stall, where wife Maeve and I shined him up again with brush, comb, and glossy spray, and tacked him up to show him off to the passing salegoers. The auction was soon to begin, so I led him out into the bustle of the sale grounds and mounted. Trailers were still being unloaded, and men and women were busy doing things with horses. Predictably, Smoky's head shot up, he got wild-eyed and snorty, and he danced and fidgeted. I was having a hard time controlling him.

They called, then, for the sellers to line up with their horses. I managed to ride Smoky over and take our place. He immediately got stirred up and hard to manage. He absolutely was not going to remain calmly in that line. To try to settle him down and buy a little time, I ducked him out to an alley between the pens some 10 or 15 yards away, where I rode him in tight circles, left and right, and in loops of a figure eight, trying to distract him, but he grew ever more unruly, and seemed at the point of "losing it" and blowing up completely. Maeve, afraid for my safety, began calling, "Get off him, Dick, get off! It's not worth it!" Getting off would be a hard thing for any old horse breaker to do, in his pride, and dismounting a horse that's charging around out of control isn't easy to do physically, either.

Suddenly, the ring boss, noticing what was going on, took a few quick strides and grabbed my horse by the bridle cheek and conducted us into the ring. I leaned toward the auctioneer to provide that brief introductory description we always give. "He's pretty green," I declared.

The auctioneer, calling to the audience, softened these words to something like, "He might be just a little green."

"No," I called back, "he's really green," and I proceeded to show off my colt. Smoky then performed the best that he had ever performed in his short life. He walked and trotted calmly, and I was even able to canter him around in small circles in that large ring. He stopped and backed at a light touch. I side-passed him a couple of steps each way (I always started them early on this important movement).

*Smoky then performed the best that
he had ever performed in his short life.*

The bidding opened with a bang, at a beginning figure that I thought would be the ending, and it leap-frogged upward, hundred after hundred. I truly thought I was misunderstanding. The increments were reduced, and the sale was finalized at somewhere right around $1,800.

Back at Smoky's stall, Maeve rejoined me and we exchanged expressions of astonishment at what had just happened. We had sold the highest selling horse of the sale that day, by far, of his kind and class.

I have often wondered, these several years, about Smoky. If his training was continued, persistently, and especially if he was kept on one farm or within one certain physical setting, he might have become accustomed to his surroundings and quit seeing all those spooks. I hope that somewhere, someone might be enjoying this exquisitely beautiful animal. Paraphrasing that other auctioneer, mentioned earlier, they might not be riding him every day, but they'll be looking at him every day. I hope that what was counterfeit for me might have become sterling for somebody else.

A Silk Purse from a Sow's Ear

It was at another auction in Missouri, ten years ago or more. Wife Maeve and I had come north to the big draft horse sale at Columbia, Missouri, a three-day, mid-winter event. For myself, I didn't need an excuse to be there. To me, these big horse auctions are far more entertaining than a concert, and you don't need a high-priced ticket. But we did, in fact, have a purpose. I was still breaking a few colts to harness, and I was keeping an eye out for a calm, steady horse to team with them in a three-horse hitch. We had lost Sparky, our good old part-Belgian breaking horse, to sand colic.

I have always liked the Clydesdale horse, the odd one among draft breeds, with its Roman nose, its hairy white legs, and its showy action, but I have never had one among the purebred and mixed-breed Belgians, Percherons, Morgans, and grade draft horses that I have owned and worked.

We arrived at the sale and began strolling through the alleys and the pens alongside them to get an idea of the offerings. We came to an animal that caught our eye.

I have always been attracted to the odd and unusual in equines, though this inclination is at odds with my thinking and my standards as a horseman, and has occasionally led me astray. The animal that had attracted our attention was indeed odd. She was a Clydesdale, a breed that I have suggested is unusual by nature, but this mare was unusual even within the breed. She was not an exemplar. Slab-sided and narrow, she was a little ewe-necked and her head—well, it was Clydesdale in spades. She was quite light for a draft breed, of medium height, with too much white on her body, but she was a Clyde all right.

She showed a little rib, but of greater concern than her poor condition were her feet. Overgrown and splayed out, they were far too long in the toe and low in the heel, with large cracks starting to spread at the edges. The man with her in her stall—he seemed to be the person representing her—thought she had maybe been ridden a couple of times, and that she was a four-year-old. I mouthed her and he was correct.

This mare had only one thing going for her—she was quiet and she appeared absolutely, unflappably gentle. And then, she was a coveted Clydesdale.

Long lines of horses would be selling before that mare, so Maeve and I went to the lunchroom for coffee and a snack. We had two or three other horses under consideration—among them a Brabant that I ardently desired—but the talk kept turning back to the Clydesdale mare.

Price is always a primary consideration. Our balance at the bank was comfortable enough for everyday purposes, but not for large purchases. "She'll go cheap," I said to Maeve. "Among all these fine horses, and she is in such poor condition and so ordinary in every way, she might not bring more than $250 or $300." The gamble, I pointed out, was in those badly overgrown hooves, but I thought I could bring them back with calculated, persistent trimming. We agreed we would go as high as $400, or maybe it was $500, and we were confident we would take that mare home.

Some time that afternoon, our mare was led, under a Western saddle, onto the dirt floor of the large indoor working area just outside the auction ring. Maeve and I made our way through the numbers of men and women busy with their horses and through the many onlookers to take another look. I walked slowly, on a cane, for I have been often crippled in accidents and had but recently healed up several bones broken in a runaway.

The man with the mare again assured us how gentle she was, and, trusting him, as well as my own evaluation, I asked if I could ride her, just to "feel her out."

"I'll need your help," I told Maeve, and handed my cane to someone. I attempted to mount, but the mare was too tall for a half-crippled old man, and partway up I faltered. I kept trying to pull myself up by the saddle horn, and the mare didn't move a muscle. "I can't make it," I puffed to Maeve. "Yes you can," she insisted, and this powerful lady put a hand on my rump and with one hard push, boosted me into the saddle.

Once there, I felt fine and picked up the reins. I noticed then that a little knot of onlookers had gathered around us and had been watching this spectacle of a gray-haired woman in a skirt helping an old man struggle up the side of an odd-looking mare.

With the loose ends of the reins, I encouraged the mare forward out around the scattered crowd and among the few horses. She felt as though she had scarcely had any bridling at all, no flexing left or right, but she remained calm as a stolid ox. I managed to keep her moving and threaded her through and

With one hard push, she boosted me into the saddle.

among the other horses. Folks kept circling around and watching, and asking questions, mostly of Maeve and the man who had brought the mare.

And now, dear readers, enjoy with me a little laugh at myself. For lo these many years, I have relished the memory of those folks watching the horsemanship of an old man, yours truly, handling a green horse masterfully, but as I have been writing these lines and recounting this story to Maeve, she has expressed surprise at my naiveté, gently informing me that, "No, Dick, what they were watching was a green mare letting a lame old man climb up her side, then quietly carrying him around amidst all that bustle. They were watching the mare, Dick, not you."

After 10 minutes or so of ambling around, I rode the mare back to her attendant, dismounted, and Maeve and I went to the bleachers to wait and watch, to bid and buy, then bring the Clydesdale mare back home to Arkansas.

Meanwhile, a young Amish man entered the ring with a refined, well-built young Clydesdale mare, a rich bay with all the proper white points. He rode her astraddle, then standing on her back. She sold for about $800. Another Clydesdale, of comparable quality but not ridden or driven, brought a somewhat lower figure. We knew our mare would go dirt cheap.

Directly she entered the ring and the bidding began. We didn't get our mouths open. Bidding started where we had planned to stop and quickly spiraled up through $1,000, ending somewhere about $1,200.

Metaphors come to mind: "Beauty in the eye of the beholder," "... a silk purse out of a sow's ear," "... shot ourselves in the foot." But the saying that best sums up what happened that afternoon was pronounced by Maeve—"Dick," she said, "you showed she was so gentle, you sold that mare right out from under yourself."

First published in Rural Heritage *December 2022/January 2023, pp. 20-24.*

Seeing the Pain of
Animals with a Child's
and with an Adult's Eyes

Author's note: This piece was adapted from a column that I wrote back in 2010, for a now-defunct local newspaper in Elkins, Arkansas, called the White River Valley News.

An end-of-the-year picnic was always a big occasion at the little one-room schools, for children and adults together, with a big pot-luck lunch and games afterward like the three-legged and potato-sack races. But that May day in Minnesota, mid-1940s, a cold rain had settled in and driven us inside.

Dashing to the outhouse, I stopped on seeing that my friend Calvin's father had parked his big truck and gone into the schoolhouse to enjoy the food and company. Within the slatted, roofless cattle rack a bunch of old ewes, newly shorn and looking naked, shivered dismally on their way to market, and it was well over 100 miles yet in that open truck to South St. Paul.

I watched those sheep with a child's eyes and suffered with them, but society was to convince me—almost, anyway—that my eyes were seeing it wrong. I was farm-raised and farmers have to be practical. The animals, we assumed, were put here for our own use and pleasure at our own disposal, and besides, we told ourselves, they didn't really suffer quite like us.

Oh, some were a little different. Dogs understood many of our words and even shared our stove on frigid winter nights. And horses answered to simple commands and shared our work in the fields (although even our work partners were sold for slaughter after the tractors came in).

Most farmers and ranchers object to wanton cruelty, and for the most part our practices were, and are, as humane as could be convenient. But it's a rough 'n' tumble world, and market prices don't allow for expenses other than the absolutely necessary, so even many of our standard practices are needlessly harsh.

Calves are castrated, and branded with hot irons, and ear-marked (notches cut with a knife) and de-horned, all without anesthesia. Pigs used to have rings punched into their noses, an especially painful operation, to keep them from rooting. Horses are tripped, thrown, have a foot tied high or their feet tied together. And lest anyone think that I'm here to condemn, let me confess that I've been there, done that—all of the above.

Sitting here now I can think of about 15 different rope hitches, most of them mild, a few more severe, that I have used to train, restrain, or subdue horses. I justify the restraint by pointing out that it is always used as reasonably and gently as possible and always with the aim of making the horse into a useful animal that can enjoy the care and protection of a long life with its human partners. As for the painful castration of calves, etc., well, some consumers buy their meat by contracting directly with farmers to assure that the animal be raised and slaughtered as humanely as possible, and they are willing to pay the price.

It's almost impossible to be human without sinning against our fellow creatures. The deprivation of liberty, the alterations by surgery, the forced labor, and ultimately the taking of the creature's life are certainly not things we would wish for ourselves. Yet these are the sins of our species, if sins they be, shared by all humanity, for our very civilization has been based on the exploitation of animals. And each of us who lives and works with these powerful animals must inevitably accumulate our own particular record of offenses and regrets of conscience.

It's easy to be kind-hearted sitting in your easy chair, but let a cow kick the milk-bucket flying and lash you in the eyes with her whip-like tail, or strain your hands and nerves to get that horseshoe set just right and the first nail driven, only to have the foot jerked violently away, sending you sprawling, and if you aren't tempted to curse and strike back, you're more virtuous than I.

So, I'm a sinner too. And yes, I still eat a little meat, and I have butchered, and I used to work horses, sometimes pretty hard, until I was in my 80s. But still, after a long life of 90+ years lived closely with animals, I'm seeing them again with the sympathetic eyes of a child, and I think I'm seeing it right. That heifer stumbling about with the pink eye acts just about how I would act with an eye about to rupture, and those steers that broke in one January day and huddled together on our front porch didn't like the cold any better than I.

The wild tomcats that have materialized like phantoms out of the woods in the winter and adopted our barn for warmth, food, and eventual affection seem to have made the same decision you or I might have made.

Like children, colts quickly become eager to get into the barn for a snack and to escape the herd for a nap in the privacy of their own stall, and I recently watched as my special saddle horse, Toby, after the first shock of his life by an electric fence, paced about, studied a moment, then twisted his neck around and with his teeth gingerly retracted the steel pan from under the fence and cheerfully munched the contents. These animals, they can't do math or write sentences as I can, but as for pleasure, pain, and lust for life, I can't see much difference.

Treatment of animals has become a hot issue, with diametrically opposing views. There are those who eat no meat or eggs and even disapprove of keeping pets, while others seem to think anything goes.

The state of Ohio recently secured criminal convictions for cruelties in a slaughterhouse the details of which I doubt this

paper would print. Arkansas now has a law penalizing cruelty to animals, and I heartily approve. But no law can substitute for our holding ourselves and each other to a standard of basic decency. If we are going to eat the flesh and eggs of these animals, and drink their milk and use them for work and sport and whatever, then it seems clear that we have a moral duty to protect them from grave physical harm, to provide adequate nutrition and to shelter them from extremes of weather, and when it comes time to end their lives, to do it painlessly and without terror.

First published in Rural Heritage *February/March 2024, pp. 62–63.*

Among the Animals Part 1: Love, Courage, and Tears

I confess. I'm an animal welfarist. But then surely you're an animal welfarist too. At least, it is very, very likely that you are. Few individuals are against animal welfare, but the devil is in the particulars.

What is ideal in our treatment of animals and what is merely acceptable and subject to judgment? And what is unreasonably cruel and should be beyond the morally and legally permissible? There are many questions, and the answers to some of these questions will be, or should be, in black and white, while in other cases individuals will measure differently. So let me remind the reader that early on in this series of writings I warned that I might drop in an occasional opinion. In this present article and in the one to follow, I will take a close look at these animals with which our lives are interwoven, and I will offer some suggestions as to how we might improve our relationship, to their betterment and our own.

I will not be self-righteous. I, too, was raised in a rural culture that valued the life of an animal only insofar as it serves our own. I, too, have committed many sins against the animals, for which I keep trying to atone. I once dehorned grown cattle with that guillotine-type dehorner that cuts the horn off close to the head and leaves blood spurting everywhere. I have, in the distant past, "euthanized" inconvenient dogs. At the riding events, when a bull was twisting in the chute and making it impossible to get down on his back, I have, like other riders, jabbed him in the hump with a spur to make him bellow with pain and jump forward against the boards in front, in order that space would appear on each side and I could jump down astride him. (I continue to be, by the way, a staunch supporter of the rough-stock riding events. These animals are very well cared for and lead good lives.) But some of the practices that I carried out when I was younger—practices which were considered standard and routine—I would not now perform. Maybe it's just that I'm old now. The poet John Sparrow has written:

> *Insensibly, ere we depart,*
> *We grow more cold, more kind:*
> *Age makes a winter in the heart,*
> *An autumn in the mind.*

Yes, it is true that with age one grows less passionate, but age has also provided me with decades of experience dealing with animals. I have been, nearly all my adult life and until recently, a horse breaker and a horse trainer, but I have also raised cattle for the market, and hogs, chickens, and goats for home use. And, of course, a long succession of dogs and cats. All these years I have been watching and observing, almost as interested in the daily dramas of their lives as in their usefulness to my own. And through all these years of watching, the conviction has grown that their lives, mentally and emotionally, are not much different from our own, we their human cousins. Michael Pollan, the contemporary writer on food and agriculture, seems to have come to a similar conclusion. He writes, "One by one, science is dismantling our claims to our uniqueness as a species."

Throughout the past few decades several naturalists have supported Pollan's view. Konrad Lorenz, in his *King Solomon's Ring* (published shortly after World War II) describes, among other phenomena, the diving of the jackdaws and their swift flight aloft again, above the roofs of Vienna. In his view, there is no logical explanation for their antics other than that they are just playing, having fun in the wind. Jeffrey Moussaief Masson, in his *When Elephants Weep*, offers many examples of intelligent and emotional behavior among elephants, as well as among other species. And, of course, we have Jane Goodall, who lived among the chimpanzees and describes so vividly their lives and habits. Especially intriguing is an account by Richard Louv, in his *Our Wild Calling,* in which he describes the attempts by an animal behavioralist, Con Slobodchikoff, working with a computer scientist, to develop a program by which they could translate the language of prairie dogs into the language of humans. Prairie dogs, Louv reports, are a very sociable species, with a vocal system for transmitting specific messages—for instance, warning whether the approaching intruder is a thin brown coyote or a dog.

The animals in these books have been fascinating to read about, but our domestic animals are just as interesting, and it is toward them that my focus is directed, for it is with them that our personal concerns most lie. We raise them and kill them for their meat. We eat their eggs and drink their milk, and eat cheese made from that milk. We make leather from their hides. They carry our bodies and pull our wagons and plows. We exploit them in vast numbers, and their lives, generally, are at our disposal—their fate is in our hands. These are thinking, feeling beings over which we exercise such awesome responsibility, so shouldn't we get to know them, as we dictate their fates for better or for worse?

To put a face on the creature, to look more closely at these animals over which we hold "dominion," I have selected a few anecdotes drawn from my observations and my experiences with animals over these past several decades. My stories are usually about horses, since that's where my life has been, but here I'll fit in a few tales about other species as well.

Horses fall in love. Any old teamster will tell you that a team worked together for awhile get as nuts over each other as a mare and her foal, and as distressed when separated. And mares can fall for geldings. Isabeau fell hard for Moonburst, our main harness horse at that time, a 1250-pound Morgan/Belgian cross. I had purchased Isabeau, a very tall, solidly built American Saddlebred mare, along with her sister Belle. Belle was smaller but bullied "Beau" mercilessly. She once chased her right out over the top pole of my solid five-foot-high corral. Beau just meekly took it all. Then one day I brought Moonburst down from a different farm. Beau took one look and swooned. When Belle the bully approached, Beau wheeled and put thundering hooves to her sister's ribs with such ferocity that Belle never again dared to go near her and her beloved.

Do my readers know that cows can cry? I have seen it often. When I was a boy, I lived and worked on a large farm (large for that time and place). From spring until fall, at milking time, the 30-some Holsteins would be herded into the barn and guided into separate stalls, where their necks would be enclosed within free-swinging stanchions. Sometimes the procedure would get confused, like when two cows would get into the same stall or another cow would refuse to put her head through the stanchion, insisting instead on going alongside. Really, it shouldn't have been such a big deal, but one worker that we had on that farm for years would become very emotional when things went a little wrong and would yell and curse loudly, and would strike and kick the cows. Then the cows' eyes would grow large and their bodies would grow tense and quiver and crystal tears would roll down their black cheeks.

Animals can show concern for others. My dogs go everywhere with me in my pickup. Last Sunday, as I often do, I took them down to Springston Ford on the White River, to let them run freely along the paths and the meandering streams that make up that section. They had gone their separate ways, as they usually do, but little Otto the dachshund came back first and climbed into the truck to sit silently on the middle armrest. A neighbor pulled onto the gravel and stopped to visit and I started to move my pickup closer. The instant I started the engine, silent Otto jumped to my shoulder and barked loudly in my ear, and he kept barking until I noticed that his buddy, Bonnie Jo the heeler, was returning, and I let her into the truck and all was well. Many of you readers, I am sure, could tell similar stories of intelligent communication by your dogs.

Otto had appeared, a stray, in our barn five years ago, at first growling at me, then quickly appointing himself as my personal bodyguard. He weighs 13 ½ pounds. He frolics with children or anyone, but if a person suddenly approaches or embraces me, even my wife Maeve, he is at the ready with warning growls and bared teeth. A couple of days ago, I was sitting in a chair by my small garden, Otto in my lap. Maeve was clearing the border of weeds and Johnson grass with a weed-eater. When she got within five or six yards of where I was sitting, Otto suddenly leapt off my lap and charged the snarling machine. Maeve whipped it away and Otto came back to my lap. I was puzzled. Maeve again started the engine, and again Otto attacked. I was mystified, until Maeve pointed out, "Why, it's clear, Dick. He's protecting you." There was no other explanation, and it's the only time I have ever seen the fulfillment, in the flesh, of that old country expression, "He'd fight a buzz saw."

In the 1950s, the Stillwater River, roaring northward out of its gorge in the Beartooth Mountains (the highest in Montana), gushed its torrents of foaming water across the pastures of the Beartooth Ranch, dividing east from west. One of my duties, working at this guest ranch at 17, was to wrangle in the horses in the morning, to be ready for riding by the "dudes" later that day. Sometimes the horses would be to the west of the river, sometimes to the east, sometimes on both sides.

Crossing the torrential Stillwater was out of the question, for man, for horse, and probably for elephant, except at The Ford, where the waters opened widely and grew calmer. Directly below this ford, however, the channel narrowed abruptly into The Chute, where the violent white waters churning over boulders could suck a horse in and toss it about like a matchstick, head appearing and disappearing, then hooves and tail, before discharging the terrified animal into calmer waters downstream.

That summer, the Beartooth Ranch had purchased four horses from a neighboring ranch. Now, horses taken from one setting and placed in another will, like Americans abroad, band together, even though they might not have been especially chummy in their native herd. These four horses quickly formed their own nuclear family.

The waters of the Stillwater were at their highest. It was about the Fourth of July, peak snowmelt time. These new horses, unlearned in the currents, crossed The Ford too low and were swept into The Chute—heads, hooves, and tails appearing and disappearing over and over again amid the boulders and foaming waters. A large black horse was cast early upon the shore. He struggled to his feet and wheeled and bent his neck and muzzle to the churning waters, following the course of his companions, nickering softly, in obvious concern for his friends—nickering, perhaps, to encourage them. They all got out okay.

I even know of an inventor among our farm animals. Ol' Jack, our faithful chore donkey for many years, sired several little mules before we had him neutered. But those mules didn't have much to do, and the pasture was small, and they got bored, and ya' gotta have fun! So Ol' Jack invented the stick game. He would grasp in his mouth a fallen branch or a stick of wood and thrust it toward the muzzle of one of his little mule offspring until he had induced it to seize the stick and run. Then he would chase it, and the other mules, having learned the game, would try to chase and seize the stick from one another. I had never seen this game played between equines before, and apparently Ol' Jack's invention died with him.

The chicken, the lowly chicken, is the animal probably most common to our rural experience worldwide. It is found in barnyards and backyards everywhere. But the chicken was once an exotic. It originated in India and Southeast Asia, where it was domesticated from the wild jungle fowl. My wife Maeve keeps a small flock, "to keep the ticks in control," she says, but—whisper, whisper—I think they're mostly pets to satisfy her deep maternal instincts. I should point out, though, that they are pretty wild pets.

These chickens are not of one of those plump and docile breeds that you can easily pick up and carry around under your arm. Maeve's chickens are mostly of the skittish bantam type, with maybe a little game cock blood mixed in.

Maeve had a hen that hatched out three chicks on the front porch of her artist's cabin, but a fox quickly killed the mama hen and two of her chicks. Maeve took the survivor indoors to raise in her cabin, where it quickly began hopping and perching on human knees and shoulders and getting into people's food, and, of course, pooping everywhere. One day, as the chick perched on my knees, I was struck by her raven-black plumage, without a point of light from beak to tail to black feet. "Quoth the Raven, Nevermore," I said, and the little bird became Poe, after the poet.

After five or six weeks, as I remember—who keeps a calendar on these things?—Maeve turned Poe out with her little flock. The libidinous rooster charged to leap on her, but Poe, not yet nubile, rushed toward Maeve for protection. Maeve quickly stooped forward and Poe leaped into her cupped hands.

Shortly afterwards, Maeve had to leave for a few weeks and I was left in charge of her poultry. With me, Poe was sometimes coquettish, sometimes standoffish. But one day, when the rooster charged her again, with one quick leap she landed on my head, her clawed feet clutched to my thinning hair. Now tell me,

*What in Poe's jungle-fowl
past inspired this move?*

dear reader, what instincts coming out of her wild jungle-fowl past had prompted Poe to leap for help from a human being? It seems to be the quick-thinking behavior we might expect from one of our own species, but not at six weeks.

Poe now struts around the cabin. She tweaks Maeve's dress begging for milk. She sends my otherwise fearless dachshund cowering under a chair. She presides.

Do animals think, have thoughts and emotions, feel pain? It's a question deliberated by some few philosophers and scientists. It's a question unworthy of serious consideration, a question perhaps immoral in the posing. Of course they think, feel, suffer pain! They have eyes like us and they see; they have ears and they hear; stick them in the ribs with a knifepoint and they'll whine, squawk, squeal, or bawl, like you or me. If we rush at them with a scary object they flee in fear, even as you and I. So by what reasoning do we and the animals march together to a sudden dividing line, where they, on the one side, remain mechanical robots while you and I, on the other, proceed with spirit and soul?

My superb all-purpose saddle horse, the American Saddlebred Hot Tabasco (Toby) needed to be fenced into his own private pasture. Electric fencing works well with horses (but please avoid that cheap, almost invisible fine wire for fencing). Animals do have to be introduced to electric, though, or they might accidentally tear your fence up before they learn how it works and how to respect it.

I think Toby had a thought that day ...

I took Toby out to the new fence, strung with that highly visible wire that looks like white clothesline rope. I placed a pan of sweet feed closely under the fence, on the opposite side from Toby. He reached for the feed and immediately got zapped in the neck. Some horses, first shocked, "freak out" and tear things up. Toby just stepped back and kept his eyes on the feed pan. Again he tried for the feed, and again he got zapped. Now he stepped back and stood quietly, considering. Then he twisted his head and neck sideways, and, gingerly avoiding the electric wire, he grasped the pan with his prehensile lip, pulled it under the fence to his feet, and munched the contents, unconcerned. Maybe he couldn't spell the word "pan," but I think Toby had a thought that day.

* * * * *

P.S. Sadly, I must write a postscript to the above story. The little hen Poe continued to thrive in our home, strutting around and intruding on family gatherings during outdoor meals, making of herself an amusing nuisance. She laid a few eggs and began setting, but a banty hen took over her nest and hatched the eggs for herself. One day Poe disappeared, and Maeve found her dead under an overturned canner kettle. She had obviously leaped to perch on the rim, and the empty kettle had flipped over, trapping her inside, where the heat from the sun bearing down on the dark blue metal had killed her (quickly, we hope).

The death of this little hen, in such a manner, casts a pall over our thoughts whenever we remember her ending, and we are left considering that if Poe had been hatched into and raised in one of those long buildings housing one hundred thousand chicks, she would never have become the little personality she became. On the other hand, any one of those hundred thousand little yellow chicks, raised in our household, might become another Poe.

First published in Rural Heritage *April/May 2022, pp. 42–47.*

Among the Animals Part 2: Toward a Common Creed

We've been visiting, dear friends and readers, through these pages for a couple of years now, beginning with some practical advice on the business of teamstering, then shifting into more personal accounts of my adventures and misadventures with our large farm animals in pasture, corral, and rodeo arena. Today I'd like to talk earnestly about just the animals themselves, and our relationship with this not-so-other world with which our lives are so closely interwoven.

Let's review a little. In the preceding article, we saw that horses fall in love, and we learned about a horse that showed grave concern over the safety of his companions. We watched abused cows cry, and a little dog try to tackle a machine to protect his friend—myself. A quick-thinking chicken leaped to humans for protection from its own kind. We saw a horse figure out how to deal with an electric fence and a donkey invent a game. Clearly these are thinking, feeling beings, not the insensate objects as they are so often treated.

The world of humans has always been one with that of the animals, going back to the days when many of our species lived mainly by hunting or fishing, and coming forward through domestication of the ox and the development of field cultivation to the days when millions of horses worked in American fields and cities, and now to present times when vast numbers of cattle, hogs, and chickens fill our pastures and crowd our pens, barns, and various "houses." I consider our treatment of the millions of animals that we process through our factory farms and slaughterhouses to be one of the supreme moral concerns of our times.

Despite our journey together throughout the millenia, humankind has worked out no generally accepted, binding creed to govern relationships with our non-human fellow creatures. Primitive peoples seem to have had a closer connection to animals than we moderns. Certain of the African Bushmen, for instance, believe that the hunter should have a sympathetic relationship with the animal they are going to run down to kill and eat.

We moderns are all over the scale in our attitudes and treatment. We Americans pamper our pets and in 2021, we spent about 99 billion dollars last year on dog and cat food, beds, toys, and trips to the vet. (We love our pets. I spent my tiny slice of the 99 billion too.) According to one real estate association, about one third of first-time millennial home buyers (people born in the 1980s to mid-90s) report that having space and freedom for their dog was a key factor in their decision to buy that first home. Meanwhile, millions of hogs, equally as intelligent, equally as needful of space and freedom, spend their lives crammed without relief into crates and pens where they can hardly turn around. Or not turn around at all. Some go crazy from the confinement.

Any person, incidentally, can decide whether they want to eat the meat of an animal that had to go crazy to afford us the pleasure of its flesh, for increasingly we have the alternative of buying meat from private farms raising free-range animals.

Naturalists and animal behavioralists are ever more insistent that these non-humans are not unfeeling objects, but have thoughts and feelings much like our own. We who deal with these creatures on a daily basis don't have to be convinced. It's only common sense drawn from our own personal experience. A growing circle of voices are calling for kinder, more sensitive treatment of all animals. I want to add my voice to that circle.

Maybe together we might work out some well-defined set of ethical principles that we can commonly agree upon.

I hope to help stimulate and keep alive this conversation about animal welfare that we should all be having, especially we rural folks whose lives are most closely involved with those of the animals. I have called this a conversation, and a conversation is a two-way, give-and-take exchange, so I urge readers to share with me their opinions on the ideas expressed in this article by writing to the editors at *Rural Heritage.*

I touched earlier upon the matter of factory farming because no one can get into the subject of animal welfare, food production, cooking and diet, ethics, agriculture, whatever, and ignore the matter. And lest anyone misinterpret my attitudes as being somehow anti-farming, let me point out that raising animals under the more natural conditions of pasture, field, and barn is much more in keeping with our rural traditions and ways of doing things than the way things are done in industrial agriculture. A team of horses can be the effective source of power on a small farm but they can't do much to supply a feedlot.

During this particular discussion, I want to talk about the animals that are directly under our care, usually in small numbers, and point out some of the things that we might do, or refrain from doing, to give them good lives and keep them from needless pain and suffering. Let's get into cases.

I have a strong feeling that no horse, mule, or donkey should be castrated at home in the corral by a country practitioner, without anesthesia. I've had one castration at home, a donkey, done by a cowman who was good at it, but I had a hard time watching the agony of that colt and I have always since had this surgery performed by a veterinarian, who puts them to sleep.

Castrating young calves—that might be different. In the distant past, as a very young man, I did lots of baby calves with a horse, a rope, and a sharp pocket knife. They were often just a few hours old, or at most a day or two. And if you do it quickly and let them up they just switch their tails and shake their butts and run right back to mama, with no signs of lasting trauma. Older, more mature animals—that would be different. But calves, there's really no need to castrate them at all. They will dock the bull calves a few cents at market time, but you haven't had to take the trouble to castrate or feel the repugnance or pangs of conscience at putting the knife to live flesh. And hey! folks, at what price conscience?

If we are going to have pasture-raised beef, we need a system for identifying ownership in some situations, like in the big pastures of our West. The traditional system, having come down through the centuries from Spain and Mexico, is branding. I can see that some animal-rights people might object, but I find the practice to be an acceptable trade-off. I used to run a small herd here in the Ozarks, on my own pastures and on odd bits of rented pasture here and there, and I branded. The fences were usually bad and the cattle strayed and I was on horseback half the time, keeping them rounded up. I once would have lost two nice yearling heifers to someone else's claim had they not been branded. The main thing, while branding, is to have a red-hot iron and stick it on them fast, so that it sears the hide quickly but superficially and leaves a light tan mark that peels. It's an iron too cold, applied too long, that burns the flesh. Where herds are small and fences tight and owners recognize their animals individually, there is no need to brand.

It has been suggested that ear tags might be an alternative to branding. I don't believe so. Ear tags, in my experience, and in any herd I've owned or cared for, have been used to identify individual animals, for health and breeding records, not to identify ownership. The animal must be confined so the numbers can be read, and a tag can tear out, taking a chunk of ear with it. The best method down through the centuries for permanently establishing ownership has been the hot brand. If the brand was well done, a cowboy could ride by and identify the animal at a glance.

As a really old "old-timer," I find myself a little out-of-touch with the latest everyday practices, but I am informed that Radio Frequency Identification (RFID)—use of a microchip implanted under the skin of the animal—is the ID system of most growing popularity.

As I say, if we are going to eat beef and raise cattle, there are certain procedures that we almost have to carry out. Take the matter of dehorning. Those horns are pretty but in crowded situations, like around bale rings or in trucks while being shipped, horned cattle can bruise each other badly. In dehorning, as in all things, we should try to do the least possible harm and cause the least pain, walking the line somewhere between the ideal and the practical.

I know of three different methods of dehorning: you can apply caustic horn paste to the little emerging bud of a horn on a newborn calf; on older calves with budding horns that are still soft, you can use the Barnes-type tool that scoops out the young horn material, a procedure that is painful for the calf but apparently only briefly; more mature cattle can be dehorned with that guillotine-like dehorner with long handles that looks like a bolt cutter. This last method is pretty gruesome. The tool cuts the horn off close to the skull to remove the fleshy growth ring. The head is opened up so one can look through the hole where the horn was and see the pulsating membrane in the sinus below. Blood spurts everywhere and the animal bellows in pain. I dehorned my first little herd of maturing steers and heifers this way, but after performing once this bloody, barbarous action, I never did it again. I decided there are some things that one animal, ourselves, simply have no right to do to another animal. Since then, when I've had to deal with a mature horned bovine, I've put it in a headgate and tipped the horns with a saw, taking them back as far as I could without getting into the painful quick, perhaps two or three inches.

By far the best way to dehorn is with the paste. Of course, one can avoid the problem altogether and raise polled cattle, but some of us like breeds that don't come in a polled version.

One minor activity that has nothing to do with agriculture but is part of our traditional rural ways in some areas is trapping. In the part of Minnesota where I grew up, with its wild woodlands and many swamps, the young men trapped in the winter for their spending money, mostly for muskrats. Opportunities to earn were few and I used to wish my friends luck, but now I feel strongly that snapping the steel jaws of a trap shut on an animal's leg is another of those things that no one should have a right to do. The leg is injured, often broken, and then held painfully as in a vise for hours or a day or more.

By the way, I have caught several pack rats in a homemade live trap of wife Maeve's design, after they had gotten into the kitchen, the bedroom, and once into a dresser drawer, and then "re-homed" them in a favorable environment far from the house.

Returning to matters of more immediate concern to farmers, I want to express another strong opinion: I am absolutely against the practice of docking draft horses' tails. Cutting off an essential part of an animal's body, the fly swatter, and throwing it away is simply wrong, and the reasoning behind this practice evades me. Presumably tails are docked to show off the heavily muscled hindquarters, but the muscles bulging on either side of a heavy groomed tail are even prettier to me.

I purchased a tall Percheron stallion with a docked tail many years ago at the Waverly sale in Iowa. During fly season, he would fight the flies so constantly with his mouth that he would lose weight, even on good pasture. Both hip bones would turn into raw sores from his teeth biting at the flies and bumping on those bones.

At the big draft horse sale in Columbia, Missouri, some years ago, I heard an older draft horse man pointing out that the Amish don't dock tails, so by docking, a breeder eliminates a large part of their potential market. Docking the tail seems to me a harmful practice with nothing to be said for it and everything against it. And by the way, the Quarter Horse people show off those muscled hindquarters by trimming their horses' tails, artfully pulling a few hairs.

I have offered some opinions here on matters about which I feel strongly, but sometimes the issues are not so clear. Sometimes it's a question of good, better, best, where best is ideal, but good is very adequate. Take the matter of tie stalls for

You don't have to cut off the tail to see the muscles.

horses. I don't like them, though I have used them myself when I've had no other choice. They restrict a horse's movement to scratch or to fight flies, and they impose upon the horse the boredom of immobility. But for draft horses they have been used in the northern states for generations, and who can say, in a place like my native Minnesota, that a horse would rather be out in the wind at thirty below?

Nevertheless, I much prefer box stalls. So why use tie stalls at all? Well, space. A tie stall 5' X 10' occupies only 50 square feet while a box stall 10' X 10', for the average-sized saddle horse, takes up 100 square feet, and the 12' X 12' stall recommended for a large draft horse takes up even more. Now, for a small saddle horse or pony, I consider an 8' X 8' box stall adequate and far better than a tie stall. Whatever your stabling system, if your animal is not worked or ridden it should have a large lot or a pasture where it may be turned out frequently for exercise.

Excellent plans for building stables, corrals, etc., can be had from your county agent or from materials published by the U.S. Department of Agriculture. I have before me, for instance, U.S.D.A. Handbook 394, by M.E. Ensminger, which contains helpful plans for building a small horse stable. I built an amazingly efficient set of corrals for working a small herd of cattle for a stock farm I once managed, following plans obtained from the county agent.

But many of us, with maybe a couple of horses or just a few cows, and probably working a full-time job, may not have the time or means for much building. Don't let the perfect be the enemy of the good! There is a lot you can do, easily and cheaply, for the comfort and health of your animals.

When I think of shelter for farm animals, I think of three things: protection from north winds; from cold rains; and from a hot sun. Just good protection, not better or best, can often be very adequate. A simple roof, made of galvanized roofing and

The horse "pavilion"   *The horse "veranda"*

supported by posts provides complete free-choice protection against cold rains or a blazing sun. A roof like this can be built even more easily as a lean-to against an existing barn or shed, where it will provide even more protection.

Horses or cattle learn immediately to use and enjoy these structures. One day several years ago, when I still had a large band of horses, I heard the pounding of a thousand hooves, and looked out the barn door to see my 12 or 15 horses come galloping madly out of the pasture to stand under the horse pavilion shown here. Split seconds later, a heavy sheet of hail came driving in behind them. Those horses had kept that roof fixed firmly in their GPS.

Shelter from a hot sun is as important as shelter from the other elements. Cattle seem to be even more sensitive to the heat than horses.

I must make it clear that I am writing from Northwest Arkansas. Conditions vary greatly. We're not exactly the sunny South here—temperatures often get down to the single digits and sometimes dip below zero—but facilities that serve us well in these climes might not be adequate in more northern latitudes, where a tighter barn with four walls might be necessary. The roughest weather we have here are the sometimes long, cold winter rains, which are harder on livestock by far than falling snow, and just a roof where they can stay dry will keep most of them comfortable and well.

In a place like Nebraska, where I worked for four years, the main threat from the weather were the stiff northern winter winds. The ranchers built windbreaks out of galvanized roofing to shelter the cattle. Just a single wall, no roof. Maybe the stock weren't snug and cozy, but those simple structures probably kept a lot of them from freezing.

During those four years I was employed by Lincoln County, working at manual labor alongside a half-dozen ex-ranch hands and small or failed farmers. These were men with calloused hands and limited formal education, but sound of mind and heart. Two of them in particular voiced the common sentiment of our little group, complaining bitterly about the investors from the city who bought up large numbers of cattle in the fall, to pasture throughout the winter on vast rented corn stubble fields, with no more protection from northern winds than the electric fence quickly strung up to contain them. "They ought to be taken to the Humane Society," our crew would grumble.

Wallace Stegner, the renowned writer on the West (the working West, not the gun-slinging West), tells of one night in Canadian history when a warm Chinook wind had blown in and melted the snows of Alberta and Saskatchewan into a deep slush. Thousands of cows, having nowhere else to lie, lay down in that slush—and never got up again. During the night, an Arctic wind blew in and froze those thousands of cows to the ground. It was by the foolishness of man, Stegner comments, that those cows were there and in that circumstance in the first place.

Our animals are at our mercy. Since we are fortunate enough to have them, while they live it is our duty to keep them free of pain and suffering and to keep them safe and comfortable. And to keep them happy if we can!

First published in Rural Heritage *April/May 2022, pp. 48–53.*

A Good Horse
or a Great Horse?

Was Moonburst a great horse or just a very good horse? Great horses can have, sometimes, great faults. The great Thoroughbred mare, Elegant Ruler, the flashiest reining horse and the most tireless long-distance traveler I've ever held between my knees, could also take a notion to try to buck me off, and once disgraced herself and me before a group of ranch hands working cows up in Nebraska. My exquisitely trained, hard-working team of big Haflinger mares, hitched to a strange wagon, ran away and smashed into a heavy post and broke nine of my bones. Moonburst, in his 28 years, never let me down. So after the following story, dear reader, you tell me: Was Moonburst a great horse, or just a very good horse?

He was foaled in 1973. The sire was our Morgan stallion Jason Allen. We had acquired Jason as a two-year-old in 1969. He became our cow horse, our kids' horse, our work horse, and then the favorite mount in our riding school. He was especially reliable in carrying his young riders "over fences," practicing for obstacles in a competitive hunter course. Jason was to go to the pageantry of the Grand National horse show in Oklahoma City, a few years later, wearing a "bouquet" in his neck, that big splotch of discolored yellow hair from his years of service "pressing the collar" against heavy loads, and he would return from that show as the national champion Morgan Working Hunter of the year.

The near horse is
Moonburst's sire, Jason Allen,
earning that "bouquet" in his mane in the
years before Oklahoma City.

Jason Allen over
fences, showing the
form that earned
him the National
Champion Morgan
Working Hunter of
the Year.

PHOTO: FROM THE COURTEAU COLLECTION

Moonburst's dam was the part-Belgian mare, Flame, an excellent worker in harness doing farm chores. Both sire and dam were of a smoothly harmonious conformation and a pleasure to look at, but somehow Moonburst hadn't put the two together very well. As a foal, he was raw-boned and awkward, and as he grew older, he didn't seem to get much better. When he was a yearling, I met my future wife Maeve, and she saw him for the first time. She had heard it said that I was a horseman, but now she questioned my credentials as such, wondering how a horseman could have bred and kept in his herd an animal that looked as much like a young moose as a young horse.

But kept him I had. It was been observed that, "Almost anyone who has horses has too many."

Moonburst grew older and stronger, if not prettier. As a two-year-old, I started riding him a little. He took me on his

... as much like a young moose as a young horse.

back without flicking an ear. I harnessed him and began dragging chunks of firewood to the house, mostly just to get him broke. He was always willing and calm.

As a three-year-old, in 1976, he was gentle and manageable enough to use in our summer riding school, but he was never a star. He was a little hard-mouthed, and with his ewe neck he would raise his head and thrust out his muzzle in response to being reined in, instead of flexing at the poll. I used him to move cattle between pastures, but he seemed oblivious to the cow in front of him. It was clear that his role, if he had a role, was going to be in the harness.

But he was getting pretty good at that. By 1977, when he was a four-year-old, our fortunes had changed and we were back to farming. When I would head him down between the rows of tomatoes or other vegetables, pulling a walking cultivator in our commercial market garden, with the lines behind my back and calling directions, he knew what he was supposed to do and he did it. Often we would come to the end of the row and he would turn back in the other direction guided only by the lines behind my back.

I built a sprayer, mounted on a wooden sled and powered by a Briggs & Stratton engine, and with the muffler popping off right at

PHOTOS: DANIEL J. KASZTELAN

Guiding the team with the lines behind my back, with Moonburst on my right.

The animal on the left, a young mare in training, is boring heavily outward with her head thrown high, but trusty Moonburst is holding her in, steadying her up, and headed straight down the furrow.

his heals, Moonburst just pulled that contraption between the rows unconcerned.

By now, he was helping break a colt or two to the harness.

The summer of 1980 was one of the driest in Arkansas history. Day after day, though the clouds billowed up in glorious display, it didn't rain and the temperatures soared above 100. Nothing grew in our large market garden.

Sitting one day with my head in my hands, depressed, I said to Maeve, not serious, really, "I feel like hitching the team to a wagon and heading to the West again." Maeve, always adventurous and ever unbound by convention, replied, "Why don't you do it, Dick?"

We sold off our possessions at auction except for a few mares that I just couldn't part with. We spent the next few weeks converting our farm wagon into a covered wagon. Maeve, falling back on her basket-making skills, split and bent into shape, from an eleven-foot white oak log skidded by Moonburst, the bows to carry the tarpaulin, the "wagon sheet." Evenings, I studied road maps.

On December 1, 1980, I harnessed up and left the hills of Madison County, Arkansas, bound for the Sandhills of Nebraska. Pulling the wagon were Duchess, a grey Thoroughbred/Percheron mare, and the tall chestnut gelding Moonburst, ever dutiful, but unremarkable.

Ten days later, at the little city of Parsons in southeast Kansas, I was hailed down by Charlie Farran, a retired construction worker, who invited me to stay in the crude cabin he had cobbled together on a few acres of pasture. This was the beginning of the wave of hospitality on which the family and I were to roll through the length and breadth of the plains of Kansas and into Nebraska.

Moonburst, ever dutiful but unremarkable. PHOTO: DANIEL J. KASZTELAN

I installed myself in Charlie's cabin for the winter, with my team in his pasture. I found a little work as a carpenter's helper and spent my spare time getting ready for our continued journey westward in the spring.

Our troupe was growing larger. Maeve and our three children (there were still only three) joined me by bus from Arkansas. My few remaining mares and a couple of colts and a gelding were trucked up from their Madison County pastures. Two of those mares promptly foaled in Kansas, and the foals would be too young to travel the road, so to haul them I purchased a small wagon to tow behind the much larger covered wagon. To help pull the extra weight, I had broke, during the winter, my fancy Thoroughbred saddle mare (Bold Ruler bloodlines—the same kitten-gentle Elegant Ruler that was to try to buck me off up there among the cowboys in Nebraska). I fashioned a triple-tree for the wagon. On May 1, 1981, we headed west.

Now I interrupt this story for a few observations on the countryside and modes of travel. How often have we all heard said things like, "You're driving through Kansas? (Or Nebraska, the Dakotas, etc.). Just give the wheel to someone else and get some sleep." How different was our experience!

Travelling at an average speed of 23 miles a day, we could much more absorb and appreciate the beauty of the land. The features of the terrain had real meaning. Starting early in the morning, our eyes would begin searching for our midday rest stop, and after that for the evening campsite. Mostly the land was flat, but sometimes the plains stretched in rolling swells, their contours seen one to the other for miles. That wandering green line of willows or cottonwoods dividing the land in the distance was not just subject matter for some artist's brush, but indicated water for the horses, wood for the campfire, and maybe some grass available. It also might indicate a hard pull for the horses after they had crossed the creek and the land rose on the other side. It was all quite dramatic.

Four horses and a mule pulled the wagons at different times, but Moonburst and Duchess were the main wagon team from start to finish of the 850-mile journey. The mule is pulling on the far left.

When I retraced our route in a pickup a year later, at speeds of 45 to 55 mph, the same land seemed as drab as others had warned. I'm not speaking of some vague spiritual feeling here—the actual physical perceptions were different.

There is more to tell but this is Moonburst's story.

We stopped awhile to break a few horses for a young rancher and we picked up an outlaw mule to break along the road. That mule, a couple of times, got our triple hitch into a tangled pile-up of hooves and harness, but Moonburst held steady.

Somewhere around Dodge City we bent northward toward Nebraska. The land was flat and the roads were hard-packed earth and the wheels rolled as easily as on pavement. Searching for an evening campsite, we pulled off onto a broad roadside acre or two along a brushy creek. Our tires sank immediately into the deep sand and we were stopped as though by a wall. We unhitched and camped for the night.

The next morning after coffee we surveyed the situation. Our horse-drawn wagon was stuck fast in the sand. We had come along the roads and through the little farm towns with such fanfare and celebration as a horse outfit that we would hate now to swallow our pride and ask for a farmer's tractor to pull us out.

I harnessed and hitched the team of three and asked them for just one more try. The mule was willing but he was still too green to deal with a situation like this. Moonburst would always give his best. The problem was Duchess. Duchess was a tough wagon horse but in a hard pull she could be balky. If the load was too heavy and she felt she couldn't pull it, if she felt she was beat, she would stop and stand as if frozen and refuse to take another step or move one muscle. It was she who had been the first to give up the day before.

Moonburst, we knew from his days in the woods, was a "solid puller." A solid puller, in the jargon of the old Arkansas loggers, was a horse or mule that you could hook to a solid stump and it would pull every time you asked. (Of course, no good horseman would ever do that.)

We dropped the little foal wagon from behind and lightened the load from the covered wagon in every way we could. The small water barrel, Maeve's cast-iron cookware, my saddle, and of course, the anvil and horse-shoeing tools—anything heavy was stacked on the ground. We dug out an extra singletree we were carrying in the wagon box and fastened it to the end of the wagon tongue. I drove Moonburst into place, linked his traces into the singletree, and signaled him forward. He threw his weight into the collar, dug his hooves into the sand, and by himself set that wagon on the hard dirt road. He had saved the family honor.

It was at that moment, I believe, that Moonburst ensured his lifelong future with the Courteau family.

Moonburst worked at various jobs, off and on, during our three years in Nebraska. Pulling the dump rake and the hay wagon, he helped put up loose hay, old-style, along several miles of Union Pacific right-of-way, to feed my band of horses and the small bunch of cows pastured by a new "homesteader" friend. The friend mowed with a small Farmall Cub tractor, and with Moonburst and his teammate, I raked the mostly brome grass hay. (The dump rake, by the way, was about the most effective of horse implements ever and the last to be abandoned. The mower was very hard on horses and was happily abandoned.)

One summer Moonburst pulled the covered wagon to give rides during North Platte's long Frontier Days celebration.

During the historically bitter winter of 1983–84, he and his new teammate, Levi (son of Duchess), sharp-shod for the ice, hauled out from the frozen floodplain of the Platte River the firewood to heat 14 homes.

We returned to Arkansas. The renter on our farm had been shot and killed (a tragedy between neighbors), so we went back to reorganize our lives and restore the farm—beginning with the fences.

With Moonburst and Levi, I was hauling in the wagon, one summer day, a roll of barbed wire, some posts, and fencing tools. I tied the team to a sapling and walked off a short distance to inspect the fence. But I failed to drop the quarter straps. When I turned around, I saw that Moonburst, fighting the flies, had kicked over a quarter strap and become entangled in the harness and was down on the ground, struggling. I tried to loosen some part of the harness to free him, but every strap was bound tight as a fiddle string.

The horse is a creature of flight. Its every instinct is to stay on its feet so it can flee. Moonburst was thrashing around frantically. I gently kneeled upon him, speaking softly with, "Easy Moonburst, easy fella." Immediately he would be quiet and I could try to find some strap to loosen, but instinct would well up and he would struggle again. Each time I would talk to him softly and he would be calm. Eventually I got him loosened enough so I could ask him to his feet and we proceeded calmly with the day's work. Moonburst was that trusting in the work partner he had known since a foal.

Moonburst's teammate, by the way, now and for the rest of his life, was Levi, the son of Duchess, who had balked in the sands of Kansas. To give Duchess her due credit, I must reveal that of the five animals that pulled the wagon, at one time or another, she was the only one who pulled it every step of our 850-mile journey, except for those few steps in the sand when she evidently thought my demands were unreasonable. Even Moonburst needed a substitute for a few days to get his galled shoulders healed.

Back on our Ozark farm, Moonburst was kept steadily busy at farm chores, hauling things: firewood (always that firewood!); hay to our new little bunch of cattle; rocks off our fields and rocks for the purpose of building; anything that needed hauling on the farm. With an antique "endgate seeder" at the rear of the wagon, I broadcast pasture seed as he and his teammate pulled the wagon. For a couple of 10-day stretches, Moonburst and Levi, and I as teamster, were contracted to pull the old Butterfield stagecoach during the annual Stagecoach Days at Springdale, Arkansas.

Moonburst had one exquisitely beautiful moment in his life. It was during that July 4th rodeo and Northwest Arkansas celebration at Springdale. Moonburst and I were contracted to pull and show off the immensely popular national country singer-of-the-day, Lee Greenwood, parading in a fancy two-wheeled cart before a stadium-filled audience. The people cheered in full throat, and Moonburst arched his neck as much as that ewe neck would arch, lifted his tail, and positively strutted. Then he went back to farm chores.

We were hired to help develop and run a large cattle farm. It was a beautiful place, here in the mountains, but much of it was rugged and inaccessible to most motor vehicles. I often used my team on this farm. The main pasture was down in a hollow so deep it could be reached only by a crooked trail so steep that the hooves of the team would slide on the dirt and the flat rock, trying to hold the hay wagon back, even with the rear-wheel brakes locked.

Either Moonburst or Levi was occasionally employed, equipped with a pack saddle and panniers, to carry tools or materials to repair the fence on some especially steep and rugged slope. The same panniers would be loaded with bags of range cubes to pour in a trail on the grass for the cows.

Farmers and ranchers were starting to feed the big round bales, and square bales were becoming harder to find. The round bales required much less labor, and, pound for pound, are cheaper.

PHOTO: DANIEL J. KASZTELAN

Moonburst and his partner Levi, laying out the first furrow.

The trouble is, you ordinarily need a tractor to handle them, and on our own farm we had no tractor. But I would have a truckload hauled in and dumped outside the pasture gate. Then with a stout rope slung around the bale, Moonburst and Levi would drag it out on the pasture and spot it where needed.

Now, I've said that the big rounds were cheaper, but I didn't say they were cheap. A bale fell off the truck one day and rolled over the bank of our steep, narrow, mile-long driveway. I brought the team to retrieve it. The bale was lodged among saplings, 15 or 20 yards below the road. I couldn't use the team down there in those narrow openings, so I tied Levi and went down with Moonburst alone, hooked to just one singletree on the end of the steel eveners. He dragged the bale up the slope, stumbled over the lip of the roadbank, and was brought to a halt when the bale pulled up against that almost perpendicular edge of the road. I thought the weight of the bale, tugging at him from behind, would make Moonburst track backwards, but he stood firm. I kept talking to him as I dropped the lines and quickly untied Levi from his sapling, leaving Moonburst at liberty. He kept watching as he held the bale.

I always worked my horses in open bridles, no blinders. I figured if I had to hide the load from them, I ought not to be hitching them to it.

I led Levi forward and the moment I linked his traces to the loose singletree on the opposite end from Moonburst's, Moonburst heaved into the collar without a signal and Levi surged forward and they pulled the bale up onto the road where it could somehow be handled.

For several months afterwards, I did not eat meat. "I will not eat the flesh of my brother," I said. I'm eating meat again, but not meat that has been raised and processed through the industrial system.

Moonburst grew older and thinner. He was 28 years old now, and was pastured, with other horses, on our farm on Pinnacle Mountain, eight miles away from the acreage where we were then living, and at a much higher elevation. On December 12, 2000 (I think—dates fade), the forecast warned of a severe snow and ice storm moving in. I raced to Pinnacle with a pickup and trailer, luckily found Moonburst quickly, and spun up the hill and out of there just in time.

Down at the small lower farm, he had access to shelter all winter, and I fed him daily more sweet feed than I have ever fed to an animal not at work.

Spring days grew warmer. A light trailer had to be moved a short distance just to get it out of the way. I chose Moonburst, instead of the younger Levi, perhaps for *auld lang syne*. He staggered a little but moved the load into place. It was the last time he was ever in harness. I took him back to the good pastures at Pinnacle and turned him in with the other horses. Moonburst had always been dominant in the herd, but now he withdrew and would stand alone. I would dismount as I rode by, scratch him, and try to give him some relief from the horse flies.

One day in July a neighbor on a four-wheeler reported that there was a dead horse in our lower pasture. His big white bones are still there. Are they a monument to a great horse or just a very, very good horse? My family, who lived with Moonburst at its core for a quarter of a century, have answered that question for ourselves, but you, dear reader, you decide the right word.

First published in Rural Heritage *April/May 2023, pp. 24–29.*

Teamster-Team Bonds

by Jacqueline Courteau

Teamsters often form strong bonds with the animals they work. Scientists might debate whether that bond is an emotion (love) or simply a learned behavior, a stimulus-response reaction (that person gives me food, so I expect positive things from them, and come to greet them in search of treats). But anyone who has worked draft animals has likely observed many behaviors that are hard to reduce to simple stimulus-response terms. When a teamster has earned the trust and respect of their work animals through kind treatment and fair and consistent expectations, a powerful bond can grow between them.

Della formed such a bond with my dad.

My dad, *Rural Heritage* contributor and long-time teamster Dick Courteau, has trained and worked many horses and donkeys over many decades (along with a few mules). He works closely with his animals—sometimes from birth, other times taking in animals that need a second chance, animals that didn't work out for neighbors or found their way into the auction ring. However they arrive in his life, he spends countless hours with each, feeding them, providing basic veterinary care (deworming, shots), caring for their hooves, training them. Working them. And there's something in particular about working together—teamster and draft animal, partners on the job, teammates—that creates a connection.

Whether it's an emotional connection or a stimulus-response reaction, that bond can be lifesaving.

Della was one of a pair of Belgian mares that Dad picked up at an auction around 15 years ago. He was already in his 70s, but he was dreaming of training up one more team of draft horses and giving workshops to demonstrate teamster skills to a younger generation of horse people. Della was a small, sweet-tempered Belgian mare with a bone deformity that caused one front foot to turn inward, which caused her to sometimes be lame (although trimming the hoof in a particular way could correct for the deformation and keep her sound). Because of the lameness, and because the team wasn't well-matched in size (Patsy was quite a bit larger), Dad got them cheap. Although they were sold as "trained," they were quite green and very spirited, and he spent many hours working with them individually. He skidded logs with one or the other, or pulled the disk, working to calm them toward teamwork.

PHOTO: BEVERLY CONLEY

Dick with Della, skidding light logs for a split rail fence.

Della and Dick returning to the barn after disking the garden.

The training program was interrupted when Dad needed foot surgery to correct a bone spur that had developed after a long-ago horse accident. The procedure was considerably more difficult than anticipated, causing intense pain and a longer recovery than the surgeon had predicted. I drove from Michigan back home to the Ozarks for a couple of weeks to help care for Dad and the horses.

At the time, his herd of 20 or more—draft animals, saddle horses, and a few donkeys and mules—was out at pasture in the rugged and rocky fields eked out of forest and dotted with bluffs and rock ledges. There used to be 80 acres of pasture on the 320-acre mountainous place we called Rimrock Ranch, but over the years, fast-growing greenbriers and dense clumps of persimmon and black locust trees had filled in edges and turned some areas into impenetrable thickets. So the horses would often split up into three separate bands as they grazed and made their way to the three ponds for water. But they would come by the house and barn nearly every day, checking the water tanks and hopeful for a nibble of grain in their feed troughs.

Della was low in the pecking order and picked on by all the other horses, but she and Patsy enjoyed the protection of a recently gelded Saddlebred, Toby, who had claimed them and another small mare as his herd, and guarded them as though he were still a stallion. The day I arrived home, the three bands of horses came up separately, and we saw all the horses except Della. Often a horse straggled behind, or stayed in the brush to keep off the flies, so it wasn't unusual for one to not show up near the barn at the same time as the others. But Della and Patsy were usually inseparable, so I did take notice.

PHOTO: JACQUELINE COURTEAU

Della's teammate Patsy, sharing a moment with Dick during one of the almost-daily check-ins at the barn.

The next day the horses came up late in the day, and we didn't see Della. So now we got to wondering, trying to figure out when and where she had last been seen.

The following day, the horses came up before noon. Still no Della. Now we started to worry and search in earnest. Despite his painful foot, Dad insisted on riding out to search the place himself, arguing that he knew the hiding places better than I would. He took a calm pony who wouldn't startle and jostle his recovering foot, and he spent hours going through all the open trails and pastures. No sign of Della.

On the fourth day, Della still didn't show up. Dad drove out in the pickup truck and made the rounds of the neighbors. Della and Patsy had escaped a few months back, and had been found grazing the rich, stream-bottom pastures on a neighbor's farm. So Dad went to that neighbor and to all the other farms nearby, stopping to ask if anyone had seen her. He returned in the early afternoon with no news.

By this time, we were seriously worried. It had been four days since Della had been seen. She was the only horse missing. Horses are herd animals, and it was unthinkable that she would just wander off by herself, without at least her teammate, Patsy.

Dad insisted that it wasn't worth riding the pastures again, since he had already ridden through them, but I was determined to do something. After all, some places were so steep or overgrown that you couldn't get through on a horse. I finally declared I would just walk the whole place. I figured I would go fenceline to fenceline, sweeping back and forth every hundred yards, until I covered the whole property in a grid, whatever the slope or tangle of brush. Dad was skeptical, but I was persistent.

I don't know why I headed down the slope first—I just went to the east fenceline, and then started down the steep hill. I walked across one narrow bench, then scrambled down a rough incline to the next. I had swept across the second bench and was almost cresting the hill to go down to the third bench, when I smelled it—a strong smell of horse. Or of something dead. My pace quickened in dread.

I got to the edge of the hill and looked down. I took in the scene: the big blonde mare, lying on her side near a tree with a large grapevine as thick as my forearm, corded and tangling around her, the ground scraped to dust by her frantic struggles. She was just 25 yards from the nearest pasture, but wouldn't have been easily visible through the brush and vines.

I ran down to see her. I knew that a downed horse is often a dead horse. Even if she wasn't dead yet, if she was hurt enough that she was down, it would be hard to get her up.

She pricked up her ears as I called out to her and approached, but didn't even try to raise her head. I came near, staying just out of reach in case she started thrashing, but she didn't have the energy. She watched me, moving her eyes only; she didn't make any other movement.

She had clearly been caught in the thick grapevine, which had rubbed deep gashes into the back of her hock and near her stifle, and the flesh was raw and torn. Even worse, in her struggles to get away from the vine, she had broken a branch of the juniper tree near the tree where the grapevine dangled, and the sharp stub left behind by the broken branch had gouged her left hind leg, deep. The wound was gruesome. You could see down to the bone.

The thing was, she wasn't actually hung up in the grapevine any more. So what was stopping her from getting up? My first thought was that if she had been there for four days, she must be almost dead from thirst. And she was probably hungry, too. I ran back up the hill, less than a quarter mile from the house, not more than 20 minutes after I had set off. I called out to Dad that we needed to bring water, food. I filled a five-gallon bucket with water, and Dad grabbed his cane and a bucket of feed and started hobbling down with me.

When we crested the hill and could see her, he called to her from a distance. At the sound of his voice, she lifted her head and nickered. He kept talking to her, encouraging her, as we picked our way down the steep slope. When we were still 20 yards away, she made a big effort and rolled so that her head was up, and nickered again. Her buddy was here—the one who always cared for her, trained her, worked with her. Her teamster. His presence gave her hope.

By the time Dad got near her—even before she drank the water, or had a nibble of grain—she put her two front legs under her, and, grunting, made an enormous effort. She managed to pull herself to a stand. Then, swaying, she took a long drink from the bucket. She nibbled some grain. Carefully, we put on her halter, and started the long, slow, uphill trek home. She limped painfully on the injured leg, and needed to stop often. But now that she knew that her teamster had come, she was willing to try—for him.

Dad spent months nursing Della's leg. After more than a year, the scars had faded and shrunk, and the hair had grown back on the scars except a couple of small patches where the gouges had been deepest. You could barely even detect a limp.

It was amazing to witness this human-horse relationship. Della's bond with Dad gave her the hope that she needed to survive—gave her the motivation to get up and try in a way that she wouldn't, or couldn't, for anyone else. I might have found her, but the bond with her teamster saved her.

First published in Rural Heritage *December 2022/January 2023, pp. 26–30.*

After hearing her teamster's call, Della made the enormous effort to struggle to her feet.

The Evolution of a Cowboy

"How do you want your steak?" the waitress asked.
   "Just rope burnt," my cowboy friend joked in reply.
"And you?" she asked. "Blood red," was my saucy answer.
   I had been, at nineteen, almost four years away from
my native Minnesota, a land of bottom-line country

PHOTO: DANIEL J. KASZTELAN

entrepreneurship where, in those 1940s and '50s, an animal's life had value only insofar as it fitted into our own. Inconvenient dogs were summarily dispatched. Domestic dogs running feral were especial targets because of the danger to poultry and sheep. On the California ranch where I was riding windmills, a little mother dog appeared. The ranch had only a few chickens, and they formed no more a part of the economy of the ranch than the sparrows in the trees. I assumed they were remnants of the flock of the ranch family that had preceded me, and they lived a feral life. But slave to the dictates of my twisted culture, I cornered the little dog in an outbuilding. She flattened in fear against the far wall and I shot her. Seventy years later, I am still haunted by her pleading face.

The superannuated Nell, a slab-sided, leaden-footed black Percheron mare, fell my lot when my first wife and I acquired our farm deep within the Ozarks in 1967. Nell continued to work as the faithful servant she had been all her life, but she soon became deeply lame. At twenty-some years, she had no future as a workhorse, but she carried many hundreds of pounds of marketable flesh and bone. Dutiful to the practical economics of my farm background, I sold her for slaughter.

I had bought the old mare, along with the farm, from Tom Dunaway, a country-raised octagenarion with very little formal education but a skilled carpenter and a competent "hillbilly" farmer. Several years after his death, his son-in-law, the then-elderly Carl Vanlandinghan, reminiscing by our woodstove, remarked, "You know, if Tom had been alive, old Nell would have died right here on this place." There was not a hint of censure in his voice but I felt humbled.

And here we come to a complexity of our life with the animals. I don't know what Mr. Dunaway's retirement plan was doing for him, but I know that his large and worthy family had been long-since raised, and that I, so much younger, was still raising a young and growing family, and that maintaining a three-quarter-ton animal on my austere, mostly wooded acres didn't fit into my cramped budget nor into the philosophy of my practical farm background.

In 1967, at the age of 34, I had moved, with my family, onto the Dunaway farm in the Ozarks, a half-section of rugged mountain acreage. Our neighbors were mostly mountain folk descended from a very few families who had migrated in the late 1800s from Kentucky and North Carolina. The older folks provided nearly all their own food off the land, growing a big garden, milking a cow, and butchering hogs in the fall. I fell into their country ways easily, for I had sat on a milk stool as a way of life growing up in Minnesota, and I had been put to work weeding the garden and later working in the field at the age of seven. I had had no experience butchering large animals by myself but my new neighbors taught me the trick, and now I had a new relationship with the animals—killing and eating them. Over the next few years, we did a lot of butchering. Maeve killed, plucked, and dressed the chickens, and together we butchered hogs, goats, deer in season, and, for different neighbors at different times, three large heifers that had been injured beyond recovery.

When we trekked north to Nebraska in 1980 in a covered wagon with our three kids and our little band of horses, we took our country ways with us and continued to produce most of our own food. We found a plot for a garden and we rented a small pasture for our horses and some milk goats, and we butchered various animals. It was there in Nebraska that Maeve and I had the disturbing experience that would affect our feelings toward the animals from that day on.

We had raised a little pig into a barrow that had grown into a large hog, too large for normal country slaughter. Maeve and I had both been busy with other matters (isn't everybody, always, in the country?), so we had kept putting off the job of butchering. Besides, with a warm fall, the weather hadn't yet turned cold enough for an ideal country butchering, and the hog weighed well over 500 pounds, maybe 600, the morning that I finally coaxed him into position for the shot.

At this point I want to make clear my attitude, and that of my family, toward the animals. We are meat eaters. This means a hog, a chicken, a steer, etc., must be killed to provide food for our bellies. But we believe that just because an animal's life is short, that doesn't mean it shouldn't have a good life; we believe that its life should end without pain or terror. We have always provided our animals with good food, shelter as necessary, and kindly treatment. When it came time to "sacrifice" (the Spanish term) a hog, I would pour a little feed on the ground, and while it was eating with its head lowered, I would draw an imaginary X from each ear down to the opposite eye and where the lines crossed, there I would plant the slug. This had always worked for an instantaneous death, painless.

The big hog, that morning, lowered his head to eat. I drew that quick X and pulled the trigger. The hog gave a short little grunting squeal, shook his head, looked up at me, and went back to eating. I quickly pulled off two more shots. The hog stopped eating and looked up at me again, shaking his head. He clearly sensed that something had gone wrong, that something had changed, and that the nice creature that had been feeding him all his life and scratching him behind the ears was suddenly no longer his friend. I had used a .22 caliber revolver loaded with long-rifle cartridges, and though this combination had always worked before, it was evident that the .22 slug, fired from a short revolver, hadn't had force enough to penetrate the tissue and bone of the large hog's thick skull. He stood still and seemed befuddled. I called to Maeve and she ran to the house for a shotgun and the hog was soon on the ground. It was a somber day at the Courteau household.

That was some 40 years ago, and I have butchered only one hog since. On that occasion we were back in Arkansas. A middle-sized hog had escaped our pen and was roaming the neighborhood. It kept rooting up an elderly neighbor's garden and she demanded that I do something. I couldn't catch it, so this time I took a heavy rifle, and though I'm a poor marksman the job went fast.

The next hog, or pig story (the terms overlap) is happier—though few pig stories, really, have a happy ending unless they are some version of the fairy tale "The Three Little Pigs." Pigs are raised for one purpose only—to be killed and eaten. They don't produce milk, eggs, or wool, and they don't carry our bodies or pull our wagons or plows. They produce flesh.

With my daughter Sarah, 13 years old at the time, I carried out a modest little-pig project 35 years ago. For just a few dollars, I acquired from a local trader seven or eight runty pigs that were way too small for their age, for they were eaten up with the mange. We immediately dipped (submerged) them in black drain oil, obtained free from a local filling station. This dipping involved a lot of catching and kicking and ear-splitting squeals, to say nothing of all the dirty clothes, but the oil smothered the mites burrowed in the little pigs' skins and they quickly turned pink and began to look healthy and grow.

Sarah and I added a little extra to our awareness of pigs and their habits that summer. We had known that while the word "pig" is spoken as a metaphor for filth, the pig in reality is a clean animal, given its choice, and will do its business in the furthest corner to keep its quarters clean. Its reputation as a dirty animal must stem from its habit, during the summer heat, of rolling in muddy wallows of its own making in its attempt to keep cool. (Our American bison have left similar wallows in their attempts to counter ticks and mosquitoes.) We were surprised, though, by another strong preference. Our feeding system was improvised. We fed our little pigs their grain out of a commercial feeder, and for water we had laid on the ground a long, low metal trough borrowed from the cow barn. The summer sun quickly made the water very warm, and the many little hooves made it muddy and foul. So what? we thought. They're pigs, they won't mind. But when, to add liquid, we brought from the nearby well a bucket of cool, fresh water and poured it into the muddy brew, the pigs crowded frantically to get their little snouts to where the fresh water was being poured. Thereafter, we emptied the befouled trough often, and our pigs got fresh well water.

When they were of market weight, we prepared to sell them. Target weight for the butcher market was about 210 pounds, reached, under good practices, at about six months. We had taken them into the cow barn to protect them from the coming winter cold. We held back two or three pigs as too small for the market, and we jostled the other four or five into a friend's pickup. Family raised, they grunted and squealed a little but loaded with little trouble. But when the pickup started to drive away, they began squealing in ear-splitting wailing, and those left behind began answering in shrill squealing also, and both groups kept up their cries until the truck was far down the road. I could think of no explanation other than that all were grieving their separation from the friends they had been together with since babies.

I know that statements like the above lay me open to the charge of anthropomorphism—that is, the attribution of human thoughts and feelings to animals. I plead guilty. I maintain that it is only through a certain amount of anthropomorphism that we may hope to understand and sympathize with our cousins, the animals.

I have, finally, a happy animal story to tell. Well, if it's not happy, it's at least not sad. It's about animal awareness. The big rooster in Maeve's flock of chickens had scratched, with his repeated mountings, a large bare spot on the back of one of her older laying hens. As Maeve stood watching her flock one day, she was amazed to see the old hen pluck straw after straw from a nearby nest and curl her neck around to place the straws side by side on her back, covering the bare spot. Astonished, and fearing she might be doubted, Maeve reached for her iPhone and made a short video. I and others have watched it and sure enough, it's just as Maeve reported. I am tempted to say the old hen did this thoughtfully, but I'll simply pass along the facts and let the reader make of them what they will.

Animals have always been at the center of my life. I have sat on a milk stool thousands of times, and ridden thousands of miles on horseback whether to tend cattle or simply for personal transportation. I've driven the big horses in the field pulling harrows and disks and plows, and I've hauled tons of firewood on the backs of donkeys. I have fed hundreds of tons of hay and silage by team and wagon to cows in four states, and have forked tons of manure onto wagons and spreaders. I've killed the animals and eaten them, and I've broke more horses to saddle than I can count or remember.

I have felt the handles of the walking plow heaving in my hands as a steady team laid out a straight furrow. I have thrilled at the great performances beneath me by the many wonderful horses I've trained. Completing a victorious ride on a rank horse in a ranch corral or a rodeo arena always filled me with a sense of elation.

The most mellow satisfaction I have ever felt with a horse was moving our little herd of cows from one rented pasture to another, along our hill-country maze of roads, riding some horse I had trained, looking back at my six- or seven-year-old daughter Jacqueline, whom I had taught to ride, riding along on a pony l had trained just for her.

Looking back, the least enjoyable part of the animal enterprise—besides the butchering (killing is not fun!)—has been hauling the young steers and heifers that we had raised to the sale barn, where nearly all of them would most surely go to slaughter. Our herds were very small and a few of the individuals would become personalities. Maeve and I both remember a Holstein steer, many years ago, that was so naturally gentle and so interested in us humans that I felt bad when I saw him chanted off in the auction ring and watched him disappear into the anonymity of the bunch headed down the alley and going off to slaughter.

I have entitled this narrative "The Evolution of a Cowboy," and you have followed the psychological course of a young man, myself, from his youthful days when he quipped, kinda cocky, about eating bloody meat, and who shot a dog because he told himself he was supposed to do it, and you have traced him, myself, into old age when I rescue beetles trying to crawl out of the sink and only kill a spider if it's a Black Widow. (I do kill ticks and mosquitoes, though, and I spray for garden bugs.) I do not believe that, even under the threat of the lash, I could now pull the trigger on that little mother dog cowering on that California ranch. And I think that, like old Tom Dunaway, I would find some way to pension off the old Percheron mare Nell.

I have tried to atone for what I now see as the wrongs of my younger days against the animals. I contribute to organizations fostering animal welfare and I seem, over the years, to have became a magnet for stray dogs. Right now three of them, fat and sleek, lie around my feet on this cold January night as I write.

Twenty-some years ago, with reports of an early storm moving in, I rushed eight miles to the pasture where my elderly workhorse Moonburst was being kept at a higher elevation, and, with ice forming on the road, I loaded him into the trailer and spun off the mountain just in the nick of time. Then I nursed the old pensioner through the winter in sheltered quarters on large amounts of special feed. Did I atone for old Nell? Or can one atone for a life taken?

Life is a struggle and a puzzle, and it's often hard to know the right way. The great Spanish poet, Antonio Machado, put it this way (the translation is my own):

Traveler, there is no road but the road you leave behind,

Traveler, the road you make, is the only road you'll find.

You make the path as you walk along, and as you backward gaze,

You see the tracks that nevermore your footsteps may retrace.

Traveler, there is no road — just a wake upon the waves.

First published in Rural Heritage *February/March 2024, pp. 56–60.*

A magnet for stray dogs.

Part 2

Other Writings

A Taste for the Ozarks

A taste for the Ozarks, like the taste for hot peppers or straight bourbon, is a taste not acquired without pain. I acquired the taste by default, leaving a land I loved to follow a job I didn't want.

I had grown up, a foster child, milking cows, pitching hay, and shoveling manure on a northern farm. Fleeing the drudgery and dreariness of that environment, but never fleeing the land and the animals, especially the horses—the horses, the horses, always the horses!—at 15 I had started gypsying into the West, working as a farm and ranch hand, a cowboy and horse breaker, and eventually a sometime professional rodeo rider. Two very serious accidents ended that way of life.

"So how did you wind up in Arkansas?" I am so often asked. The answer is easy—"Everybody has to wind up somewhere, don't they?"

So let's just fast-forward. In 1967, at age 34, I stood with one reluctant foot in an institution of higher learning and the other resting uncertainly on a mountain farm in one of the hillbilly-est counties of the nation. (Madison County, Arkansas, still has only a single traffic light.) I felt worn down by the hard physical labor since childhood, by the accidents, by the danger and bodily punishment of the rodeo years and then the long strain of studies. I was holding at bay a critical case of asthma. My life's experience had been so intense, so varied, that I wasn't seeking any more of the new and exciting. I just wanted to find a comfortable groove and coast awhile. So it was okay that I found the Ozarks kind of drab. The mountains weren't high enough to keep you oriented in your sense of direction, and the roadsides revealed mostly barren yellow clay, and though the valleys had good farm land, they are narrow so there wasn't much of that farmland. That the roads were merely upgraded wagon roads was somewhat comforting, but the stench as you passed the chicken houses lent the landscape no charm. I didn't know the people yet but I wasn't looking for new experience.

And then a tapestry of life, interwoven between the human and the natural, began to unroll before me and demand my participation until here I stand, captivated still at the age of 90.

On that September day, I had just arrived from the Shenandoah Valley of Virginia, in an old 1940s cattle truck towing

PHOTO: DANIEL J. KASZTELAN

Maeve kept a flock of chickens for eggs and meat.

a U-Haul trailer, and was still unloading my five ponies when the local savant appeared. Carl Vanlandingham immediately began to teach: "Here's a paw-paw grove. The fruit's good if you like it, but wait 'til after frost for those persimmons over there."

He immediately began to identify the rich variety of flora on our farm: "Hickory. See those crazy branches. Tough wood, good firewood, but it rots fast." "Sassafras. Leaf like a mitten. Bark from the roots makes good tea in the spring." "White oak. You can make good money if you cut it into bolts 42 inches long and sell to make whisky barrels." "Dogwood...." The list goes on. The lessons taught not only by this old sage but by the hills themselves were never to stop.

A few days after moving in I stopped along our primitive road to help a middle-aged couple having car trouble. At my inquiry the wife barked, in accents from somewhere, that they were "leaving that mud hole down there!" pointing down into the hollow at one of the most picturesque old rundown pioneer farms in the community. She was angry—angry at the mud, at the road, the ticks, the dust, the heat, the cold, angry at me it seemed. It was a drama I was to see re-enacted often, in varied format. "I've seen them come but I've never seen them stay," Carl Van would remark in his epigrammatic wisdom. I myself was later to coin the epithet, "The Ozarks, graveyard of dreams." For the opportunity of this land, it turns out, is mostly the opportunity to discover and confront one's own realities. For Sale signs abound. Historically the land has been cheap to acquire, thus easy to leave, giving a double twist to the old phrase, "Easy come, easy go."

John, a 20-year man, a sergeant, retired young from the Army. He and his wife Polly (the names are close enough) purchased their own dream place, a nice modest little house on a few acres adjacent to our own land. They were the best of neighbors, generous with their time and interesting in conversation. Hard-working and self-disciplined, they set about pursuing almost feverishly their country dream. After a year their little bankroll was almost gone and they returned to their native East Coast, where they were both to work at jobs for new funds to buy more tools and a better vehicle for our rough roads. In five years they returned, financially refreshed. Again they worked like busy ants, but their efforts seemed to find no focus other than maintaining impeccable order around their house and plot of land. One cold, drizzly fall day I found them listlessly, pointlessly raking leaves under the bluff down in their jungly woods. A few days later John appeared at our door, loaded with gifts of tools and other belongings and offering his pickup at a giveaway price. "We thought this was what we wanted," he said, "but I guess it wasn't."

We were very fond of them, so it was bewildering and sad, the first time I had seen a big bright dream grow dim and die

PHOTO: DANIEL J. KASZTELAN

I loved the curve of the neck, the flow of mane and tail.

So it has always been horses for me.

before my very eyes, and all so frankly articulated. They had lasted seven years, with only about two in residence. We, the Courteaus, were to hold on another four years before our own dreams grew troubled.

Each of us, I suppose, must be sustained in the journey by some dream. For me it was horses. I fell in love with horses the winter I was nine. It was not unlike falling in love with a woman, something that was to happen to me a lot. I loved the curve of the neck, the flow of mane and tail, the rhythmic beat of the gallop. Their gaiety and freedom was always a lift to the spirits. Most soul-satisfying of all—really!—was the plop of the hoof planted firmly at a fast walk and the snap of the pastern reaching for the next stride. Riding for pleasure and sport had been exciting as a child, and then employing the horse as a worker during my youthful cowboy days, but as I grew older,

I kept my chainsaw running.

a utilitarian son of the working classes, it was horses pulling loads that most drew me. In fact, my last job on a Western ranch had been as winter teamster. The hills of Arkansas were to allow full scope for my interests and aptitudes in this direction.

So it has always been horses. It was a humble position on the faculty of the University of Arkansas that brought me here, but it was the need for a place to keep my horses that took me out to the hills. That was the fateful move—soon the land began to reclaim her own.

In the Ozarks, I discovered, doing was more important than having, and I found more varied skills among the people here than anywhere I had ever been. A countryman here was his own carpenter, plumber, electrician, butcher, mechanic, what have you. ("How is this house studded?" a 16-year-old asked,

I learned to fix my own vehicles.

beginning a repair job.) Any "hillbilly" could work on his own pickup, even swap engines, and some could do a complete overhaul under a shade tree. Fixing and filing a chain saw was the minimum competence required. I have learned to predict almost nothing about individual behavior, but I have observed this, that if the man of the family (Sorry feminists!) can't keep a saw running to keep his family warm, they'll almost surely move out.

I immediately felt the pull of the challenge and found myself doing all kinds of things that had nothing to do with my professional work—clearing land and raising cattle, shoeing horses and breaking colts for pay, raising ponies for sale. Having considered myself congenitally mechanically inept, I now learned to fix my own vehicles and file my own chain saw. I acquired a good team, for I could not conceive of running a farm without real live horsepower, and then I let myself be talked into logging with horses. I just couldn't say no to anything. "Beware of adventitious opportunity!" is a precept I might now offer to the collective wisdom. Within four years I had fizzled and phased out of the academic world.

This history would be false were I not here to recognize, and express gratitude for, the immeasurable contribution to my life and work by the generous woman with whom I shared life's joys and burdens for 15 years, my former wife Joanna Wojtowicz Courteau. It was Joanna's moral and material support that allowed my desultory ruralization, and her support that allowed me the freedom to further develop and refine my skills with horses. It was a job in town, often a woman's job, that made the pursuit of many a country dream possible. "I'm an Arkansas go-getter," I would hear the men joke back then, a little ruefully. "I take my wife to work in the mornin' and go get 'er in the evenin.'"

Joanna and I did a lot together. Together we built the Rimrock Ranch School of Horsemanship, a small summer camp for children. But our close bond had not withstood the stress of separate interests, separate ambitions, and the physical separation necessary to keep both our rural business and the family going, so in August of 1976, after four moderately successful seasons, Rimrock Ranch closed its doors, and I found myself on the mountain with a new wife, the then-youthful Maeve Dolan, and our infant child, Sarah, the future a huge question mark. All bridges burnt behind, our only resources for support, besides a ragtag little bunch of horses on a steep and rocky tract of mountain land, were our own energies and skills. The next four years we would put to proof the supposition that, with enough will, skill, and elbow grease one could make a living solely off this unfruitful land.

The first winter was grim, and unfortunately set the pattern. I sold firewood and got into some light logging (always with

Dick and Maeve in those early days.

PHOTO: DANIEL J. KASZTELAN

horses, of course), salvaging the dying elm trees. I shod horses and hired out to build fence. Much of our food would come from gardening and our own butchering, along with milk from a cow or goat. Maeve kept expenses down by cooking basic food over a wood cookstove. She worked alongside me loading logs. The summer after we closed Rimrock Ranch we borrowed money to plant a crop of staked tomatoes. Maeve, her belly heavily pregnant, would grab the work horse's tail to be towed back up the steep trail after field work. She stopped packing tomatoes briefly to give birth to our second child, Darcy. We packed 34,000 pounds off one acre that summer and made a little money, but not as much per hour as the local girls we hired to pick and pack, for our nearly round-the-clock hours were incalculable. We still believed that horticulture, traditional in the Ozarks, could provide an alternative rural economy, but it seemed almost hopeless for one family to try to go it alone. A highly capable young couple, our fellow pioneers in the new tomato business, were struggling on a nearby farm. We suggested a limited cooperative endeavor but found no interest. Discouraged, we contracted our horses and our services to a wealthy businessman up in Missouri, but our vision didn't mesh with the ways of the wealthy and we were soon back home, too broke now to pay for electricity, plumbing, or propane. We planted another tomato crop. A third child, Amable, was born. We logged some more and we hired out but we were hitting dead end.

And then came the appeal from Catholic Father Biltz. It was 1980 and the refugee camps in Southeast Asia were spilling over. We had land, a place, so we agreed to sponsor two families, emphasizing that they absolutely had to be farmers, preferably Hmong. We thought that if anyone could partner with us to make a little Garden of Eden in the Ozarks it would be the Hmong. Everything went wrong. Of the thirteen Laotians—not Hmong, as it turned out—that crossed the Pacific under our promise only five actually reached our farm, and they were from the capital of

Taking a rest stop on the covered wagon trip.

Laos, citified through and through. The two men stayed cheerful enough but they wanted no part of farm work and retreated indoors from the heat. The thirtyish mother of two, on arriving, would sit beneath our maple tree and keen in piercing, cadenced crescendos. After a couple of weeks all were rescued from our dreadful rurals by a compatriot in Dallas. As their departing plane rose Maeve and I, exhausted, nerves shredded, looked at each other with eyes a little bleary from celebratory whiskey and burst out, in one voice, "Let's get outta here!"

And get outta here we did. We left—none of this seemed as crazy in practice as it now sounds in print—we left on a horse-drawn covered wagon headed north.

We came back, though, four years later, and as I stepped out of the truck and almost kissed the ground, I realized that only in absence had I become an Arkansawyer. It was late evening, May, and the atmosphere was heavily perfumed with the scent of blooming locust trees. A whippoorwill sang and the vibrato of

PHOTO: DANIEL J. KASZTELAN

One of the children following the plow, looking for bugs and worms.

those darling little tree frogs filled everywhere. Purplish clouds, laden with moisture, were rolling in from the Southwest and the air was almost palpable.

I have loved every place I've been, as long as it wasn't a city. The lakes and birches of my native Minnesota are clear and clean, the soils of the Red River Valley are black with fertility, the Western plains crisp in their feel and the Rockies overpowering, but only here at the 36th parallel does Mother Nature turn voluptuous.

We returned, Maeve and I with our children, to become fully engaged again with life in the hills, but looking back it's clear that those early years—1967 to 1980 for me—were the most intense and essentially "Ozarkian" of the Arkansas experience. The memories come flooding:

- Looking back, from my saddle, at seven-year-old Jacqueline, my daughter and Joanna's, riding her pony behind me, patrolling our scattered pastures for cattle.
- Watching the children, Maeve's and mine, padding along in their bare feet in the smooth damp furrow behind the plow, picking up bugs and worms.
- Loading firewood with my boys, who, though indifferent to the horses, were always glad to see them hitched to the wagon when the wood had to be hauled out of some hard place.
- Watching Maeve, my young city-bred wife, explore the country ways, processing meat, baking bread in a wood cookstove, making white oak splints and baskets.

The quintessential experience of the twentieth-century rural American male was working either with machines or on them. I feel no nostalgia for the endless hours spent bending cramped muscles over an ailing engine, or changing flat tires, or getting knuckles skinned trying to free rusted bolts. This mechanical stuff could go on for days, painful disheartening days, but what would make it all worth the effort was getting to

PHOTO: BEVERLY CONLEY

Maeve carving wooden spoons.

go back to work with the horses again. A child of the working classes always seeking some use for horses other than sport or war, some justification, I've known the thrill of watching my powerful horses snaking a log out of the woods and down a bluff, have known the sensual gratification of guiding the wooden handles of a one-horse cultivator as the dirt folded over the roots of corn and tomatoes. I've been able to return, for awhile, to ways I wish had never vanished. Horses have nearly taken my life many times, but I suppose they've had the right, for they have given me my very life. They've been the wellspring of whatever energies I've had for anything, including caring for the family.

The farm in the Ozarks was a fine place to raise a first family, and second family, and then a loving composite family. After

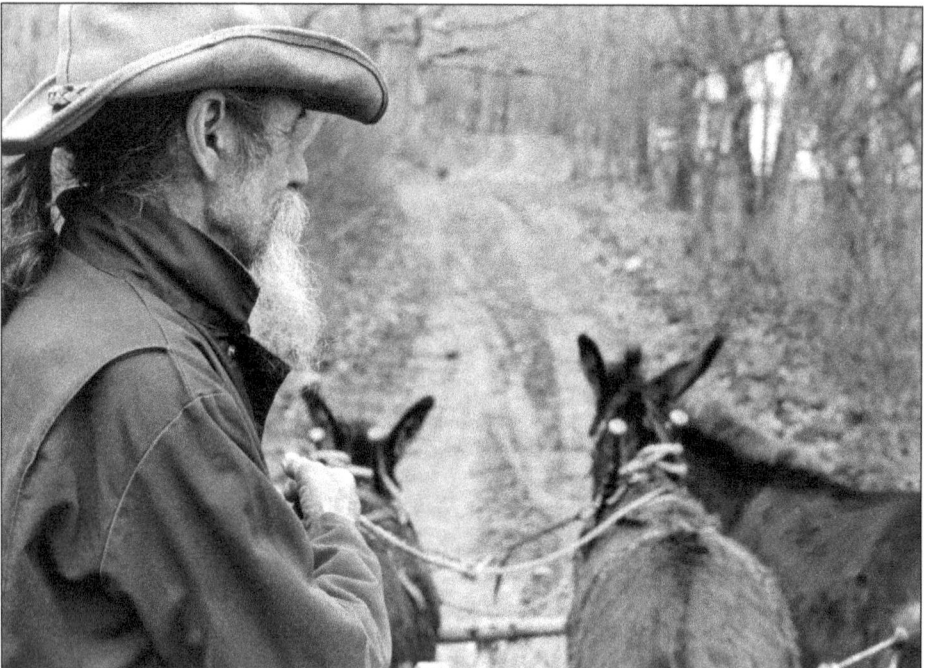

PHOTO: BEVERLY CONLEY

There's an alternative to fossil fuels.

PHOTO: DANIEL J. KASZTELAN

A playground for the children in the Ozarks of Arkansas

Rimrock Ranch, I always hoped we would work up another rural family business, something that would keep at least a few of us working together and close. We did make a couple of efforts but nothing jelled. Building a big rustic shelter around an old mobile home on a few acres close to town, as a family center, is as close as we got.

Though none of our children have chosen to follow my footsteps as a horseman nor Maeve's as homemaker and craftsperson, growing up they all had to work and they've gone into useful occupations, teaching, writing and editing, skilled mechanical work, photography. One, the brilliant Amable Casavant, is off drugs and out of prison, a hard-working laborer fostering a small family.

In the Ozarks, I have seen a place where human potential could unfold and flower. Maeve looked at a pile of sawmill tailings, carved a scrap and developed from her artistically carved spoons a modestly lucrative trade. Our daughters wrote on their rural experiences and found a springboard into their careers. A son started working with me on small engines and old pickups and now has two hundred vehicles under his supervision. I came here from a commercial farm background where an animal's life or its disposal was totally at the whim of humans and have evolved to the point where I am unable in conscience to raise animals for slaughter, and I see their lives, like our own, as having value in themselves. Spiritual growth?

I have sought, in this account, not to allow the demands of telling a story to impose a coherence on the past, some sense and meaning, that wasn't there. We thought there was purpose in what we did, ideals. The horse camp—"Children need a skill to give them self-confidence." The work horses and donkeys—"Let people see there's an alternative to fossil fuels." Most especially the market gardening, work repugnant to a horseman who has known the plains—"There's an alternative to the job in town."

We have told ourselves, Maeve and I, that we were only doing what we had to do to survive, but of course at any moment we could simply have given up and gone to town for easier, safer jobs. Maybe, under all the dust and sweat, we were just playing hard at life. If so, what a playground we found in the Ozarks of Arkansas!

PHOTO: DON HOUSE

Dick and Maeve, reflecting on life in the Ozarks.

PHOTO: DANIEL J. KASZTELAN

Searching for the Sun Through Leaves of Grass: On Animal Power

with research and editorial assistance by Jacqueline Courteau

All photos by Daniel J. Kasztelan are of Mike McCormick and Horses at McCormick Work Horse Farm in Ohio, unless otherwise noted.

The jingling of trace chains is a gentle sound, cheerily soft and unobtrusive, like a muffled musical background to thoughtful silence. The chains are attached to traces, which are attached to hames, which are strapped around the collar—the horse collar, that device that harnessed the power in grass and grain and changed the history of the world. Thousands of men and women yet living were born into the quiet surroundings where only a jingle of chain, a creaking of leather, and the plodding of hooves marked the flow of power from beast to burden, from the collar to the wagon, to the plow, to the harvester or to the construction implement that sustained their world. Almost as softly as the sun's rays from which it rose this energy flowed—and make no mistake, that's what it was, solar energy but little removed.

The sun's rays fall upon growing green plants, that through the process known as photosynthesis reshuffle the carbon, oxygen, and hydrogen contained in air and water to form the carbohydrates of vegetable tissue, thus making an energy cell of every plant. Voilá, stored solar power! Horses—and oxen, camels, water buffalo, elephants, donkeys, etc.—eat grass. Also

The hames are strapped around the collar. PHOTOS: DANIEL J. KASZTELAN

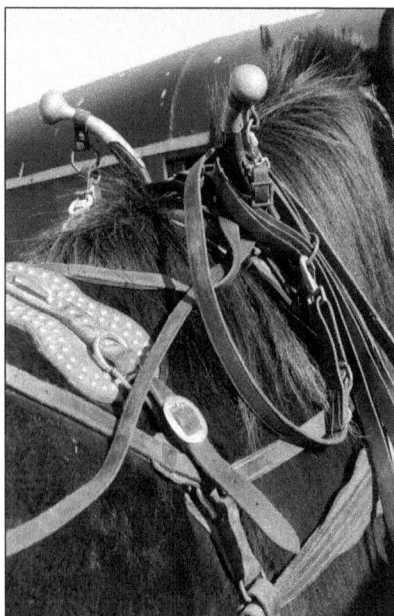

The hames.

PHOTO: DANIEL J. KASZTELAN

Horses and other work animals eat local—grass, hay, corn, oats, rather than oil—to gain energy for locomotion.

oats, corn, barley, wheat, rye, spelt, emmer, sorghum, clover, alfalfa, molasses, sugar cane, ragweed, and some tree leaves. Camels eat thorny plants and shrubs, and the hard-working donkeys on my farm eat the noxious cocklebur. All this stuff these animals eat, even the cocklebur, makes them strong and full of energy. Lots of that energy is available for locomotion, and part of that locomotion has been used to power civilization since its beginnings six or eight thousand years ago right up to the days of my youth.

All civilizations must be based, ultimately, on agriculture, and the Eurasian civilizations that came to dominate the planet were inseparable from their draft animals. Whoever has tried to raise a large garden using only hand tools and their own muscles must know that the tightest production bottleneck comes at the very beginning, when you're trying to break the land.

Once the sod is turned or the earth's crust is broken, you can do a lot with the shovel and the hoe, but that initial plowing is a backbreaker. Much less arduous, but still requiring vast inputs of energy, is the follow-up procedure of harrowing, further refining the seed bed. Even with the land well tilled, prodigious manual labor is still required to raise and harvest a field of corn, wheat, turnips, or sugar cane, but getting those clods turned and broken up—that's the big one. So when the ox was first yoked to the plow, it must have been not only a revolution for humanity but transformative in the individual lives of all who labored in the land.

The ox, by all accounts, is a marvelous work animal— strong, patient, calm, willing, and slow. He requires no harness, only the rudimentary yoke, and, when well-trained, is managed mostly with the voice. He's an animal well-suited to what I reluctantly term a "primitive" technology, and for several thousand years, this stalwart pulled the plows of mankind and drew the heavy loads.

The horses of northern Europe are heavy-boned and muscular, and some time in the 800s, the Norwegians devised the horse collar, which, resting against the shoulders instead of the neck or breast, allowed the horse to throw his full weight and strength into the job. In a couple of hundred years, horses were pulling plows all across northern Europe. From the 1500s onwards, with this newly harnessed horse power, coaches and carriages were transporting passengers in and between the growing cities as Europe and England began to bustle—but that's somebody else's story.

Out on the farm, the ox continued to hold sway, although evidently there was considerable competition between the ox and the horse for pride of place. Medieval documents provide

PHOTO: DANIEL J. KASZTELAN

That initial plowing is hard, even with a good team like Moonburst and Levi, working with Dick.

PHOTO: DANIEL J. KASZTELAN

Percherons were the first big draft horses imported to the U.S.

a comparative economic analysis of the respective advantages of the two animals. (It may seem odd that some of us can find it absolutely fascinating to learn how much oats and hay horses and oxen were eating in England six or seven hundred years ago, but that's the kind of passion you're dealing with when you get into work animals.)

In the American colonies, the ox was dominant well into the 19th century. The first big draft horses, Percherons from France, were not imported until 1839. Only with the invention of new farm machinery, which required steady speed, strength, and stamina, did the big horses begin to take over. Precision planters and drills were invented to follow the plow in getting the fields planted and sown. In the 1830s, Cyrus McCormick invented the complex reaper, which was still drawn, on the Minnesota farm where I was raised, by two big Belgians and a Percheron: Sally,

Dick, and Rex. A similar machine cut and bound cornstalks. Hay was cut by the new gear-driven mower, with its oscillating blades, and gathered by the tons using a supremely efficient, high-wheeled rake with a mechanically-powered, foot-operated dumping mechanism. Wagonloads of hay were hoisted into tall, round-roofed barns using a track-and-pulley arrangement powered by horses, and out in the field, "overshot" stackers thrust their wooden arms high into the air and slammed huge loads of hay down onto the tops of stacks.

Stationary units were developed that could be adapted to deliver raw power to a variety of machines, like those used for grinding feed, threshing grain, or expressing juice from the stalks of cane. Roads were built and maintained using horse-drawn scrapers and graders. Laura Ingalls Wilder, in her *Little House on the Prairie,* describes the almost choreographed movements of the squadrons of teams and teamsters moving

Harvesting potatoes.

PHOTO: DANIEL J. KASZTELAN

earth to build the roadbed and gradients of the railways crossing South Dakota in the 1870s. America was flexing its muscles, and those muscles were mostly animal.

We were in a horse-powered technology, but not a primitive technology. That horse-drawn reaper in my childhood cut the oats, gathered them into precisely measured bundles, wrapped the twine around them, then automatically tied the knot, cut off the twine, and kicked out the bundle. Our radio seemed to me not more mysterious. America was deeply into the Machine Age.

The machine, by one definition, is "a device to transfer, transform, or apply energy to do useful work." All a machine needs to make it go is energy—and that was the downfall for living horsepower, for that energy can come from anywhere. "The plow doesn't know what pulls it," quipped one country philosopher arguing for the use of horses. True, but the argument cuts both ways. Since it makes little difference whether the energy springs from a muscle or a piston, when the internal combustion engine came along, it was a simple step just to hitch one in front of a plow and head down the field. Refinements came later, but those first tractors of the early 1900s were most truly the "iron horses" of the day.

The engine didn't take over all at once, though. The nation that launched The Spirit of St. Louis was still fed mostly by horses. Driving through the Great Plains today, you might see, impounded behind earthen levees, large artificial ponds, each of which sometimes waters several hundred head of cattle. A friend of mine, who would now be about 100 years old, helped build some of those ponds with an earth-mover drawn by four horses. Another friend, who would now be well past 100, remembers following a wheat-threshing machine on its neighborhood itinerary with his family's team of mules, used with two other teams, walking in a circle, to turn the gears of the power unit that drove the concatenation of belts and pullies, gears, arms, and shaking screens of this big machine.

I myself witnessed and participated in the transition from one technology to the other. The farm I grew up on used both horses and tractors. An agricultural textbook I used in college, in the 1950s, still had chapters on the care and use of work horses, and the Montana ranches where I worked during those years still used teams of horses to feed the big cattle herds during winter. Here in Northwest Arkansas, we used mostly horses and mules to skid logs out of the forest until about thirty years ago. In fact, animals are still used to skid logs here and there around the nation, especially where there is concern to protect the remaining forest. Of course, quite a few horses yet work on cattle ranches. And then, there are the perennial Amish!

PHOTO: DANIEL J. KASZTELAN

Animals are still used to skid logs here and there around the nation.

So there are a few hold-overs and hold-outs, but shortly after World War II, or thereabouts, the use of animals in harness or under yoke had been all but abandoned. Americans, and most of the Western world, had simply walked away from traditions six or eight thousand years in the building. Farmers and their fellow toilers in the cities now worked to the clamor of engines instead of the clatter of hooves. Across the Atlantic, Dylan Thomas had written his doleful verse, "The Ploughman's Gone":

> *Man toils now on an iron saddle, riding*
> *In sun and rain over the dry shires,*
> *Hearing the engines, and the wheat dying.*
>
> ....
>
> *Man who once drove is now driven in sun and rain.*
> *It is the engine for companion.*
> *It is the engine under the unaltered sun.*

At farm auctions, buggies sold for as little as fifty cents. Harnesses hung useless on their pegs, and those old wooden-wheeled wagons stood rotting in the fields. Big Percheron and Belgian work horses were sold for slaughter by the thousands for 25 dollars or less, including gentle Sally, Dick, and Rex. Some farmers were saying that soon you'd have to go to a zoo to see a horse.

A dozen years before I was born, the United States was the most self-sufficient of all industrial nations. With our variety and abundance of natural resources, it's hard to think of a single item truly critical to the national well-being that we did not or could not produce within our own borders. (The folks at Starbucks might protest, but surely our great horticultural alchemist, Luther Burbank, could have figured something out.)

Even rubber for our tires we could produce synthetically when supplies were threatened during World War II. We had coal for steam, and rural America was powered mostly by its 26 million horses and mules, with another 2 million working in the cities. But to deliver our energy we had chosen the engine, and we have fought wars to keep that engine running. We seem committed to a foreign policy of assuring access to oil by whatever means. The problem is, other nations want that oil, too, just as the availability of cheap oil seems to be coming to an end.

Energy, with its concomitant environmental issues, is the topic of the times, and political careers are beginning to hinge on environmental stands. In the early 2000s, as macho a Republican as Arnold Schwarzenegger turned into a political coquette as he flirted between big business and the green vote. Renewable, sustainable, and alternative are the catchwords of the day amidst dire warnings of "peak oil" and "petro-collapse."

Wind power, solar power, hydrogen, and nuclear power are being variously proposed.

Why don't we just forget about ethanol, that problem disguised as a solution? Raise corn to feed it to cars? You gotta be kidding! (One recent analysis has suggested that it takes more energy to produce a gallon of ethanol than the energy contained in that gallon—which is also true of petroleum-based gasoline, but the conversion to ethanol is even less efficient. Whatever the efficiency debate concludes, however, raising corn to produce ethanol still generates environmental costs associated with how it is grown.)

Jared Diamond, in his recent book, *Collapse*, warns of the potentially fatal consequences of too much dependence on other societies for critical resources. Might this be the proper moment for an anachronistic nonagenarian like myself, who has spent a lifetime apologetically trying to hold back history in his own little corner, to step forward and suggest that—couldn't we at least talk a little bit about horses? After all, we haven't separated ourselves from the animal kingdom even now, not at all. We still hunt them by the millions, eat them and milk them, force eggs from them, and pet them, on a scale unprecedented in history.

Indeed, it is remarkable that there has not been a broader discussion regarding the radical shift in the course of human affairs caused by the abandonment of animal power, for it would be hard to conceive of any single historical event more revolutionary to everyday life. In its far-reaching consequences, it seems almost comparable to the introduction of agriculture itself. This has been no simple change, like switching from steam to diesel, or growing soybeans instead of cotton. For countless millions, the adoption of the engine has determined not just how we do our work, but what kind of work we actually do, where we live, how our day is structured, what leisure time we have, and how we spend it. It has undoubtedly driven up the divorce rate and helped fill the prisons. Young males have been especially hard hit. In my day on the farm, we began working shoulder-to-shoulder with the older men at an early age, and, with lots of kidding and camaraderie, we were quickly welcomed into an adult society that needed us. Professor G.F. Warren, a Cornell University agronomist, reflects on the sociological aspects of working with animals in his 1910 publication, Elements of Agriculture:

> The extensive use of horses has had a great influence on our national character and history. The boy who trains a colt gets a lot of training himself. It makes a man expand as he learns to manage a spirited horse.

There must be upsides as well as downsides to this social upheaval, but in my 20 years just inside the borders of the academic world, I never once heard the topic discussed, neither in nor out of the classroom, and I know of no major novelist who has directly taken on the subject as a central theme. Charlotte Brontë bestowed literary fame on the machine-smashing Luddites of 19th century England, but it was only through incidental mention by a children's author, Laura Ingalls Wilder, that I learned of those teamsters who refused to contract their horses to build the railroads.

If horse power has failed to arouse much interest as a sociological or literary topic, as a subject for consideration as a partial solution to our energy-pinched prospects, it's an absolute non-starter. There seems to be a solid resistance to acknowledging animal power as a serious topic even for light conversation. It goes like this.

You're enjoying lively company over drinks among friends of like political persuasion, who share your dismay at how consumerism, corporate greed, runaway technology—all that stuff—are ravaging the environment and heating up the planet. All agree that oil and the engine are principal agents in this catastrophe, so you suggest that—just possibly?—might a partial return to animal power, on a limited, case-by-case basis, in agriculture at least, take some of the pressure off? Your friends fidget and avert their eyes, then change the subject. Recently, one staunch environmentalist acquaintance assumed I had to be talking about harnessing methane gas. Her line of inquiry might be more congruent with the times than mine, but I forge ahead.

PHOTO: DANIEL J. KASZTELAN

Might a partial return to animal power in agriculture help reduce planet-heating fossil fuel use?

So, just what can a horse do? Well, it can't outpull a tractor. Horses, huge though some might be, can only get just so big (3,200 pounds is the record), while tractors can always be built bigger. Indeed, a direct comparison would be fatuous. New technologies are so refractory. Initially intended, usually, simply to make a given task easier and faster, they escape control and lead us down the many unknown paths of unintended consequences, where we find ourselves not just doing things differently, but doing entirely different things. A case in point: With the powerful new tractors and other big machinery, farmers can cultivate hundreds or thousands of acres. So they must now cultivate them, working longer and harder than ever, at a job the essential nature of which has been transformed. Those thousand acres might require spreading a half-million pounds of commercial fertilizer. (I remember the first bags of fertilizer that were brought to our farm, when I was 14. It made me uneasy. We had used only manure before. Now we were dependent on something from the outside. The cycle had been broken.)

Rather than pitting the horse against the tractor in a tug-of-war, it would seem more relevant to start by measuring the horse against the work to be done. Could horses farm the farms and feed the people? Just what can a horse do?

Animal scientist F. B. Morrison reports that "[i]n 1935 Rock and Tom, an Ohio team, weighing a total of 4,450 pounds, pulled the dynamometer the full distance [of 27.5 feet] when set at a pull (or tractive resistance) of 3,900 pounds, establishing a new world's record … [T]he champion pull … would be equivalent to starting a load of more than 25 tons for 20 consecutive times on a good pavement."

Professor Arthur L. Anderson, of Iowa State University, estimated that one work horse was needed for about 25 or 30 acres of land to be cultivated, and stated categorically that a farm should have more than 75 cultivated acres before

PHOTO: DANIEL J. KASZTELAN

Spreading manure: Work animals keep it local, generating natural fertilizer at no added cost.

replacing horses and mules with a tractor. Since the average-sized farm, mid-1940s, consisted of 174 acres, with about 58 of them cropland, it is clear that, under his recommendations, there wouldn't have been a rush to motorize.

Anderson is rich in objective criteria. He suggests a ratio for equivalences: 5.5 horses equals 1 tractor (at that time), or 2 horses for 1 truck. He calculates the feed required: per horse, about 1.7 acres of hay and 4.2 acres of oats or 2.5 acres of corn.

Another means of achieving perspective would be to view turn-of-the-century (19th to 20th) agriculture against its historical past. Warren puts the matter in sharp relief:

> In 1830 it required an average of three hours of time for each bushel of wheat grown; in 1896 it required ten minutes. In 1850 it took four and one-half hours to grow,

harvest and shell a bushel of corn; in 1899 it required forty-one minutes. This saving of time has been due to the substitution of machinery drawn by horses for human labor.

It should be emphasized that figures like the above were not the musings of cracker-barrel oracles. The U.S. Department of Agriculture and the land-grant colleges and universities conducted very extensive research on farm plants and animals, even delving into such abstruse scientific problems as a comparison between the efficiency of the horse, as a motor, and the tractor, in converting fuel into available energy. The tractor won in the raw data, but Morrison was highly favorable toward the horse in his interpretation, pointing out the obvious: One was fed hay and grain, crude fuel, while the other required refined gasoline.

These agricultural scientists examined and measured everything: feed consumed; therms of energy produced; work performed; oxygen inhaled and carbon dioxide exhaled; protein, vitamins, and minerals required; possible choices of feeds (a couple of unusual choices would be potatoes and hominy for horses? and how about carob tree seeds and dried fish?); yearly hours worked by horses and the hourly cost of that labor; even the value of their manure, not an inconsiderable sum.

Much of this research from two continents (in Europe they were busy, too), well over a hundred studies in the chapters on horses alone, is summed up in Morrison's *Feeds and Feeding*, that voluminous compendium appropriately bound in black—the stockman's bible. One of the more interesting studies reported by Morrison was conducted in 1929 for the USDA on 735 corn-belt farms, comparing the costs of keeping horses on three different classes of farms:

1) those that worked horses in traditional teams of no more than three animals;

2) those that worked horses in the new big-team hitches of four or more; and

3) farms on which a general-purpose tractor was used for part of the work.

Forget the dollars-and-cents figures they came up with. What startled me were the acreages. The farms using the smaller teams cultivated an average 137 acres of cropland with 6 horses; those using a tractor and 4 horses farmed 196 acres; but those using only horses in big hitches were the largest farms of all, tilling an average of 252 acres with 11 horses!

Could horses farm the farms and feed the people? Apparently, they could in 1929.

Let's pause here. How big is an acre? Slightly smaller than a football field, 43,560 square feet. Get your mind around that one. Farming 252 football fields with horses! I don't want to go back to the sickle and the scythe either, but for my purposes, we had come far enough. In fact, with those big multi-horse hitches we had probably already come too far.

Even as that 1929 study was in progress, though, horse farming was in decline. Maurice Telleen, in his wonderfully humanistic how-to manual, *The Draft Horse Primer,* sketches the unequal competition from 1920 to 1945 between the horse interests and the big machinery companies. He details how the financial world and the information establishment of the Midwest favored the big, new, motorized machinery. Engineering input into horse machinery ceased, and then even its manufacture was discontinued. This is critical, for the immense power of the horse is only raw power, useless until effectively channeled.

Despite the countervailing winds, some agricultural professors seemed decidedly if diffidently unenthusiastic about motorizing. This should not be surprising. They were students of the living, not engineers, and they cautioned a go-slow approach. Their advice went mostly unheeded. This should not

PHOTO: DANIEL J. KASZTELAN

The immense power of the horse is only raw power, useless until effectively channeled.

be surprising either, economic choices being based, so often, more on desire than on the ledger. The animal advocates had numbers in their support, but for all the counting and weighing and measuring of hours and dollars and pounds, of energy, breath, horse feed and excrement, in the end, their arguments fell back upon the less-ponderable.

Even Professor Anderson, he of the ratios and recommendations, is finally reduced to perplexity, conceding that, "some of the advantages of either [the horse or the tractor] as motive power are difficult to appraise." He then goes on to enumerate the relative points in favor. All advocates of live horse power, whether writer-farmers like Maurice Telleen, animal scientists like those cited above, or rural dwellers like myself, put forth much the same arguments.

We all like the horse's versatility. He is an endlessly adaptable power unit that can be "plugged in" to perform a surprisingly wide variety of tasks. On the same day, you might haul a load of feed up a steep muddy hill to unload at the barn, where you pick up a few bales of hay to take out to the cows, bringing back a load of firewood. After lunch, you move some trash and maybe plow the garden, then split the team and drag some poles out of the woods with one of them while your wife gives the kids a ride on the other.

The horse's performance is affected little by mud or snow, and cold-weather starting is never a problem. They also tolerate heat very well, but hot or cold stay comfortable in the

PHOTO: BEVERLY CONLEY

Dick and Maeve picking up a few bales of hay with a team of a donkeys.

most rudimentary shelter. They can function in terribly rough terrain, and will pull a wagon wherever the axles clear and it won't tip over.

The horse's usefulness is bounded only by our own ingenuity in devising ways to apply his willing energy. Telleen shows a draft horse unrolling telephone cable out West.

On our own farm, we once cobbled together a very successful power sprayer, with the noisy Briggs and Stratton that powered it popping off right at the horse's heels as he dragged the contraption between rows of tomatoes in our two-acre commercial field. The forecart, a device for adapting some tractor machinery to use with horses, is now being commercially manufactured.

The ultimate in adaptation, though, I think I witnessed recently in an Amish community in Missouri. This firm produces heavy wooden beams for constructing buildings. The timbers being turned out that day measured eight by ten inches thick and about 16 feet long. Running the entire length of the mill lay a heavy rotating drive shaft, around which were fitted several pulleys and belts, each supplying power to a big machine, like the huge band saw and the massive planer.

Driving the shaft and all the machinery was a power unit fabricated from the differential and transmission of a junked "semi-," the truck gearing all turned by four flaxen-maned Belgian horses.

It's the choring, though—the hauling and dragging and skidding around the farm—where the horse not only excels, but is positively superior to any motorized contraption. Small horses and mules, even donkeys, are especially handy at these tasks. In a rational world, the little Haflinger breed from Austria—a large pony, really—would have a bright future as auxiliary power. You don't need a team of Budweiser Clydesdales to bring in a few armloads of firewood. This choring, by the way, is especially profligate of gasoline if you're going automotive. You fire up the pickup a few times to jaunt here and there around the farm, and first thing you know, you're "runnin' on empty."

Of course, one of the main attractions of animal power has always been that it runs on homegrown fuel—hay you've raised yourself or maybe purchased from a neighbor. At worst, you feed grain raised in a neighboring state. In my native Minnesota, our work horses stayed fat and healthy over the winter eating the coarse wild slough grass that would otherwise have gone to waste, along with leftover alfalfa from which the dairy cows had taken the better parts.

Oat straw, another waste product, sometimes formed an important part of winter rations in those northern states, and everywhere horses have often been grazed on rough or irregular pastures that had no other use. The essential point is that they draw their energy from the surroundings, or at least from within the nation—not from Saudi Arabia or Nigeria.

Energy once used is dissipated and lost forever, but the horse returns to its surroundings the raw materials for future energy. The manure, and its critical value in maintaining soil fertility, is one of the chief reasons given by the Amish for clinging to their horse power. And then, completing this cycle of life, the last unifying link and the clinching argument for live power, are the babies. This power unit replaces itself. A mare can be worked right up close to foaling time, given a brief maternity leave, then returned to the harness. If you don't need the colt yourself at weaning time (five or six months), you can sell it to someone who does.

The argument for horses becomes stronger as lands become poorer and the means for acquiring and maintaining complicated machines grow more slender. The tools and equipment for working animals have always been cheaper, simpler, and more durable—that reaper that I described earlier notwithstanding. The anvil I bought second-hand when I was

This power unit replaces itself. Fancy the mule, out of one of Dick's donkeys.

17, and have used to shoe horses this half-century and more, has the date 1875 stamped on its side. It's not an antique, just an old anvil. Wagons and harness were passed down from generation to generation. We bought a wooden wagon up in the Bohemian country of Nebraska in the '60s with the date 1917 somewhere under its birdies and bluebells, used it hard around the farm for a dozen years, and sold it in excellent condition. It wasn't an antique, just an old wagon for hauling firewood. During the great changeover, from 1930 to 1950, capital investment in farm machinery increased 350%. It's not hard to see how a lot of small farmers got squeezed out, while others had to get bigger to survive and pay for it all. A 1977 study revealed that in a particularly conservative Amish community, farmers were spending only 5% as much for equipment as their conventional neighbors.

Much of our horse equipment has always been locally produced, by the town's harness maker or blacksmith, etc., and can be easily repaired on the farm. Some years ago, we were preparing the land for our tomato crop. A handle on the walking plow broke. Crisis! Where would we find another? My wife eyed the problem a moment, went to the woods with a saw, and shortly returned with a curved hickory sapling shaped roughly like the original handle. Breakdown time—an hour. Now there's a technology you can live with.

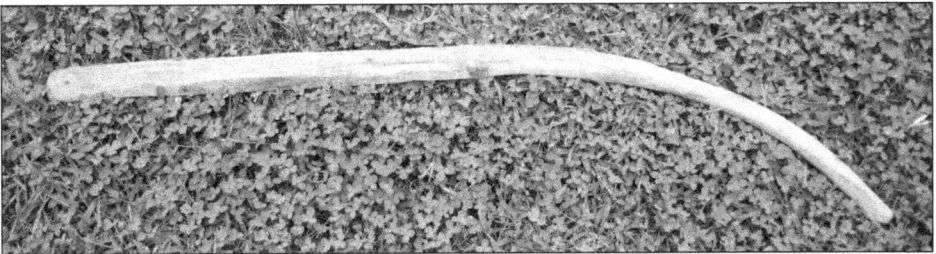

PHOTO: CALEB COURTEAU

This replacement plow handle was easily made from a hickory sapling harvested right on our place.

It might seem that a quiet, willing team of horses, a power unit drawing energy right out of the soil at its feet, working with dependable, easily maintained, long-lasting machinery, would provide all the power a farmer should need. Horse-powered agriculture circa 1900 certainly must be counted as one of the highest achievements of any civilization yet. Stand beside a great team someday, heads high above your own, massive muscles in every part. Get your hands on the lines, speak to them softly and feel those tons of intelligent power surge joyously into the collars. Feel the strength coursing back through your hands as the furrow opens behind you or the great wheels move beneath their load, and surely you will ask: And how could they have abandoned this?

But abandon it they did, and I've spent a lifetime pondering why. Why did the beautiful, exciting world of my childhood

How could they have abandoned this?

PHOTO: DANIEL J. KASZTELAN

simply collapse? There were reasons, of course, some of them more powerful than the merely economic. The reason most frequently given for converting to tractor power was an oversimplification, maybe a rationalization, but the words must be given heed: "When I stop using that tractor, it stops eating." It's a weighty argument, for, whether they're working or whether they're loafing, horses keep right on eating. The farmer must manage closely to avoid for his horses too many idle days (numerous under the best of practices), and to avoid maintaining unproductive animals. This continues to be a serious problem in those vast areas of the "developing" world still cultivated by draft animals, mostly oxen (over 50% of the planet's tillable lands, according to one source). Strict accounting, however, would have to consider all costs, not just the cost of feed.

Convenience and freedom from responsibility weigh heavily in favor of the motor. Probably more important than the cost of the feed itself is the fact that horses do have to be fed, and somebody has to be home to feed them. They require care, and, therefore, regularity and stability in the life of the family that cares for them. It takes a tight culture with common values, a disciplined and organized lifestyle. All across those northern states where I was a youth—Minnesota, North Dakota, Montana—the young men danced and drank beer on Saturday night, but the horses got fed and the cows got milked on Sunday morning.

Then, there's the inconvenience of having to harness the horses and hitch them to a wagon. That's not much if you have even just an hour or two of work to do, especially in view of their efficiency once in action, but for a short chore, it's a temptation even for a horseman just to jump on the seat of a tractor or a pickup and turn on the key. The one-horse cart can cut this hitching time to less than half, but even that is not good enough sometimes in this age of ease and speed.

The convenience factor can be deceptive, though, like many of the other advantages of mechanization. If you turn that key and the engine doesn't start, it can sure blow a hole in your day.

The greatest difference between working an animal and working an engine is that the animal gets tired. The only way to get around creaturely fatigue, in heavy field work like plowing, is to use more horses or farm fewer acres. Animal traction (the term currently in vogue) is, thus, more labor intensive. Big machines greatly increase production per man-hour—but not per acre, a fact often overlooked.

The abandonment of horses, however, probably had little to do with technical considerations and much to do with the juggernaut of history. Animal power ran contrary to the ethos of the age. Lewis Mumford, in his *Technics and Civilization* (published the year I was born), reflects upon the role of the machine in the life of modern man:

> *If anything was unconditionally believed in and worshipped during the last two centuries, at least by the leaders and masters of society, it was the machine.... [T]he service of the machine was the principal manifestation of faith and religion....*
>
> *Only as a religion can one explain the compulsive nature of the urge toward mechanical development without regard for the actual outcome of the development in human relations themselves.*

The machine as religion! Indeed, writers like Professor Anderson sound like uncertain converts, shaken in their old faith but not quite accepting the new. We who continued to work horses began to feel like eccentrics, and if we were being watched while skidding a log or plowing a field, we sensed subtly that our work was perceived not, truly, as real work, but as a kind of quaint, play-like work for show.

It was the age of the machine, and woe to the gallant horse! For he was pitted against one of the most effective machines ever built, a very icon of the Machine Age, the ordinary farm tractor. You set the throttle in a fixed position, the engine grumbles and growls melodiously as the governor kicks in and out to hold a steady engine speed, the big wheels turn, and the work gets done. And—oh! cruel inequality!—this dynamo doesn't get tired and it doesn't get hungry.

And as for you, the driver, you're in tune with the times and right with the world, and the neighbors know you're a person in full serious standing.

It's an amazingly effective machine, and, when used with other machines almost as sophisticated, as it nearly always is, the combination forms the technological powerhouse that farms America today. It's a tremendous system when it works, and for those at the top, it usually works well, or 1% of the population wouldn't be feeding the rest of us.

For a horseman arguing the merits of animal power, I may seem to have sung too loudly the praises of the tractor. Not to acknowledge its incredible effectiveness would be sheer nonsense. Yet this intensive mechanization, which, along with certain other phases of production, has been called the "industrialization" of agriculture, has come with a price. Lewis Mumford remarks that we seek "regularity, order, and certainty" through the machine. Indeed, the purring or rumbling or rhythmical shaking of a farm machine can be almost hypnotically soothing, but the net effect of a series of machines is, too often, chaos in the life of the farm family.

For one thing, tractors light their own way, so they can be worked around the clock and often are. Then, without the fatigue factor, the farmer need not conform to the natural rhythms of feed-and-water, work-and-rest that characterize farming with horses. Worst of all are the breakdowns. Any farmer, but particularly the one on the margins working with tired old machinery, knows, as he lies abed planning tomorrow's work, that his plans are contingent, that he'll bale hay or combine wheat "God willing"; for out in those machines of his lie thousands of parts, among which may be one just on the verge of failure, so that tomorrow, and maybe all next week, he'll not be combining wheat but trying to identify the source of the trouble and to extract the offending part, chasing down a replacement, maybe in another state, working to get the part re-installed and the doggone combine running again before his crop ruins.

Industrialized agriculture has performed such marvelous feats that a continuing supply of unlimited good food is almost universally taken for granted. Yet the very success of the system has obscured its underlying problems: Is it good for the land? Is it good for the people? Is it good for the animals and for living things in general? And above all, is it sustainable?

Wes Jackson, of The Land Institute (a research organization based in Kansas that seeks alternative approaches to agriculture), maintains that 90% of U.S. cropland is losing soil to erosion at 17 times the rate of regeneration. And decades ago, Sir Albert Howard warned of the harmful effect on the soil of too much reliance on artificial fertilizers. Voices are being raised in many quarters against the horrors of factory farming and the assembly-line cruelty at the slaughterhouse, together truly a holocaust for the animals. Others fear the health and environmental effects of heavy use of pesticides. All who valued life in rural society lament the withering of our villages and communities.

Massive mechanization is just one feature of modern agriculture, but it seems to be the keystone of the whole structure, the one phenomenon that shapes all the rest. Machines have taken much of the backbreaking labor out of our lives, but machines can also get out of hand and work us harder than ever.

Mechanization as we know it began on American farms about 1830, with the reaper, and only 70 years later huge combines drawn by 32 horses—as many as 50 in hilly areas— were harvesting wheat in the vast fields of the far West. The hired crew of five or more arose at four a.m. to feed, water, and harness the horses, and the work didn't end until six in the evening or later.

That mammoth combine prefigured the shape of 20th-century American agriculture, and illustrates an interesting irony—that 19th-century mechanized horse farming bore within itself the seeds of its own demise. Understandably, they soon put an engine on the monster to power its internal workings, and reduced the number of horses. Next, they made it self-propelled and discarded the horses altogether.

Meanwhile, by 1900, still the heyday of the horse, American fields were full of many smaller, simpler machines, effectively taking a lot of the physical drudgery out of farming. It's when they put a motor to the whole works that things got out of hand. The machines got bigger—lots bigger.

Farms and fields got bigger, outstripping the farmer's ability to deal with them by traditional organic methods, like manuring and mechanical (non-chemical) weed control. Monoculture became the rule. Animals were concentrated into enormous facilities where their wastes became a problem instead of a resource. The use of artificial fertilizers skyrocketed. The labor force declined drastically. And everybody seemed to be working harder. In my own hobo-like youth and early manhood, working on farms and ranches in a half-dozen states, I found an almost unvarying relationship between technological "progress" and a long workday. It's not simply mechanization that's the problem, it's big mechanization—bigness and all the complexity and vulnerability that go with it.

I'm not so quixotic as to suggest that the nation's farmers as a whole return to horses. The radical restructuring of our land tenure system necessary for such a move, and the return from the cities of millions of families ready to revolutionize their lifestyles, seem inconceivable at present. Powering agriculture with animals wouldn't even have a noticeable effect, by itself, on our national consumption of energy, for agriculture accounts for only 1% of the total used each year in the U.S. (Incidentally, doesn't that figure lay bare to the gaze the in-your-face, screw-you-Jack-I've-got-mine hubris of a species spinning wildly out of control, its focus and sense of proportion totally confounded? Only 1% for our most essential activity, growing our food! Where's the other 99% going?!)

Rather, I wish to address those few individuals who want to farm, who want a piece of the action, but who cannot, or do not want to, participate in the big technological scene. And such there will always be. For many reasons, not the least of which is all the money and all the bone-wearying, spirit-sapping labor it takes to keep a farm full of labor-saving machinery going. The big high-tech scene may work out just fine for those at the top who have survived the winnowing-out process of the last six or seven decades and are able to operate late-model machinery in top condition, but for many of those on the margins, struggling to keep going on slim funds with aging equipment, 20th-century farming has been what the Spanish historian Salvador de Madriaga called "the hell of the machine age."

Don Salvador, writing in 1947, two years after the Enola Gay, probably had in mind much darker things than a malfunctioning hydraulic system or a scrambled wiring harness when he referred to "the era of the Machine now swallowing us," but the farmer lying on his back with a cramp in his neck and grease dripping in his face, bewildered and disheartened after struggling for the third day to get the damned thing going, might find the metaphor apt.

Among the points put forth in favor of the horse runs a common thread—the liberating joy of independence. Independence from the banker, from the implement dealer and the parts man, from temperamental ignitions and carburetors, from the caprice of weather, and, above all, from the fuel pump and from the intricate supply system, now stretching worldwide, necessary to keep complex machines running. I wish I could convey to the non-horseperson the sense of quiet confidence that settles over the man or woman of the land who holds the reins of a good team with a storm moving in. Bring on your rain and snow, your rising creeks and muddy slopes; my friends and I, we can handle it come what may!

Failure in some part of an industrial system is always a real possibility. I remember the scramble to get rolling on synthetic tires during World War II, when Japan overran the natural rubber supply of Southeast Asia, and as a boy I explored the abandoned chromium mine shafts along the Stillwater River, in Montana, where the U.S. government had fostered a crash program to ensure supplies of that critical metal during the war. Could a modern, mechanized society survive a failure in a major part of its supply system?

It's a question to which we have, in one case, a more than hypothetical answer. Cuba, after the collapse of trade relations with its patron, the Soviet Union, in 1989, could no longer obtain new machinery nor parts and fuel for its by-then highly mechanized agriculture. By 1990, only 10% of its tractors were running, and the country was suffering a severe food shortage. The Ministry of Agriculture established an emergency program for the acquisition and utilization of draft animals, and to breed up the necessary ox population.

The few old men who knew how to work oxen—the *boyeros*—were sought out to train a new generation of drivers, so that by the end of the 1990s, a revamped Cuban agriculture was successfully powered mostly by oxen, and the acute food shortage was a thing of the past. Soil scientists approved, mainly because compaction had become a severe problem on Cuban soils with the excessive use of tractors and other heavy equipment. Others—among them some farmers, administrators, and economists—were less enthusiastic, seeing the use of oxen as a regression to the past, useful only as a stopgap measure. Once Venezuela was again supplying cheap oil, farmers were reportedly drifting back toward tractors. So maybe there's the shortest answer to our earlier question: Why was animal power abandoned? Human beings don't weigh the pros and cons very closely for the long term, we just do what's easiest at the time.

It is tempting to speculate on the shape of American agriculture should we, like Cuba, be forced *en masse* back to animal power. My father-in-law, a World War II veteran, was fond of quoting some obscure writer who declared, "You can't just do one thing."

A large-scale return to animal power, presently imaginable only in the event of a critical curtailment of oil supplies, would necessarily entail a train of other changes. The agricultural labor force would have to be greatly increased, so farm size would have to be drastically reduced or some system worked out for putting more people back on the land. Since commercial fertilizer, a product of the petrochemical industry, would be prohibitively expensive, our methods would have to become again almost wholly organic, with more complementary integration of crop production and livestock raising, keeping animal manures where they belong, on the farm to enrich the soil. Our diet would change, as more food would be raised directly for human consumption and less would be processed through highly wasteful (and inhumane!) feedlots and factory farms. Energy costs would encourage more production for local consumption. Arkansas, which is to tomatoes what the Mediterranean is to grapes, would no longer be importing its tomatoes from Mexico, at a high cost to quality and the environment. Several of these measures taken together might do much more to conserve energy than the small savings achieved just by converting to animal traction.

Studies on the Amish have revealed that the savings of energy in an Amish household are even greater than those that redound from the field.

A return to horses would not, just in itself, do much to stem environmental degradation. Keep in mind that American forests were razed in the 19th century by hand-powered cross-cut saws, not by chainsaws, and that the Dust Bowl was raised by plows pulled mostly by horses and mules. Horse farming should, however, lead to a closer relationship with the land, to that husbandry that essayist Wendell Berry sees in the good farmer, the conservative attitude that keeps things small enough to be closely cared for. "Cut the cloth to fit the pattern," I've often been urged by an elderly Ozark neighbor, passing along generations of wisdom earned in this grudging, fragile place. Accepting limits comes easier when you don't have your hand on the throttle.

Though agriculture eats such a tiny wedge of the national energy pie, fuel costs are, on the other hand, a close second among farm expenses. This figure could skyrocket, or, in a worst-case scenario, petroleum-based fuels could become practically unobtainable.

Among the voices warning of imminent petro-collapse is that of Jan Lundberg, who in 1973 co-founded the *Lundberg Letter,* which became the leading trade journal of the petroleum industry. I know Mr. Lundberg sounds a little doomsday, but when a petroleum-industry analyst of this stature tears up his driveway and starts riding a bicycle—well, maybe he's had a nervous breakdown, but shouldn't we at least take thoughtful notice?

The answers to the problem of highly mechanized, petroleum-based agriculture will be mostly individual, but since nothing is more basic to human welfare than food, it would seem that an intelligent government would be putting some measures in place, and I don't mean just wind generators, fuel-efficient cars, and bio-based fuels to keep the big wheels rolling under our same old lifestyle. To start with, stop paving over some of our finest agricultural lands! And, as a horseman, I have a modest proposal: We should foster the breeding of draft animals, so that we have reservoirs of "genetic material" scattered around the country for when they might be needed.

European governments long financed and presided over the breeding of horses, promoting superior lines, and we have our own precedent in the Remount program, once intended to ensure available mounts for the cavalry. (As late as 1937, the Quartermaster Corps of the U.S. Army had 652 stallions, mostly Thoroughbreds, placed with ranchers who had agreed to breed 20 or more mares annually to supply the cavalry and artillery.) There are plenty of good draft breeds and superior individuals to choose from, although it's amazing how we have let some animal resources, heritage breeds developed over the centuries, slip irretrievably away. Devotees of the magnificent Boulonnais, the most stylish of all draft horses, are struggling to maintain a viable breeding population. In fact, the lighter branch of that breed, which only a century ago was the swift, long-haul freight-horse of France, is now extinct, as is our own once-famous Conestoga horse. The Poitou donkey, one of the planet's two major breeds for raising large, superior mules, now number only about 200 worldwide. If you're going to discontinue production of an old reliable engine, for God's sake, at least save the blueprints!

Certainly, we should have programs around the country for training cadres of young workhorsemen and -women. When forced back to animal power, the biggest hurdle for Cubans was that they didn't have nearly enough oxen, nor enough individuals who knew how to handle them, and their old boyeros became a national treasure. Our land-grant colleges and universities should begin offering classes, next semester, in workhorsemanship. I submit that instruction in how to harness, drive, and care for a plowhorse would come closer than many of the things we presently teach to fulfilling the original mandate of the Morrill Act, under which the "leading [but not exclusive] object" was to teach subjects "related to agriculture and the mechanic arts."

Some forethought should be given to machinery. Fortunately, a few small manufacturers are reappearing—mostly, I believe, to supply the Amish, but also for the hobby workhorse people and a few scattered farmers and loggers who just prefer doing it with horses. Already, our vaunted "American ingenuity" and competitiveness are in play, as we manufacture and market such innovations as the forecart, and export horse machinery back to appreciative Europeans.

These initiatives would not require billions for ground-breaking research, only a little knowledge of history—very recent history—and could be put into place immediately. Even if they prove never to have been needed, their cost will have been a pittance as insurance against catastrophe. The U. S. Department of Agriculture spends nearly $200 billion a year on its various programs, of which only around 1% ($30 million) is earmarked for sustainable agriculture programs; at present, no research or funding programs specifically support or focus on animal traction.

But I suggest these societal measures only in passing, for I had proposed to address only the individual. Even if the pumps stay full of cheap fuel and the bins stay bursting with affordable fertilizer and the parts supply lines stay open from China, Mexico, and Brazil, there are those who will feel compelled to seek an alternative, and to those I would offer encouragement, and a few words of advice:

Horse power is adequate for a small farm. Machines can do some jobs better and many jobs faster, but horses can be adequate, so I suggest you avoid dual technologies, keeping high-tech machines for some jobs and horses for others. Some do it successfully, but life on the farm has always been the furthest possible from simple. Why clutter it up with more than the absolutely necessary? If you want to farm a small acreage and you like the idea of taking your energy right out of your surroundings, if you want to avoid dealing with complex machines, if you have the necessary personal self-discipline and family cohesion and don't mind being tied down, and if—absolutely above all!—you like the smell of horse sweat and the jingle of the trace chains, and if, when you've pulled the harness off your team and watered them and fed them their sun-drenched hay, the cozy munching sounds make your spirit feel that it has just settled back into its natural home, you've probably found your proper groove. Look around you. You may have joined, or be leading, a movement, and together you may someday be called upon, like the Cuban boyeros, to feed the people.

So don't bow down to the idols of another's religion and act the apologetic eccentric. When you drag that log or pull that plow, it's genuine work.

First published in condensed form under the title "Horse Power" *in* Orion, The Magazine of Nature and Culture, *September 2007, pp. 64–71.*

Dick worked with daughter Jacqueline on this article.

REFERENCES

Anderson, Arthur L. 1947. "Farm Horses." pp. 656–666 in *Animal Husbandry*. NY: Macmillan.

Asociación Cubana de Técnicos Agrícolas y Forestales, 2001. *Transformando el Campo Cubano: Avances de la Agricultura Sostenible*. Havana: Translated by Dulce María Vento Cardenas, Lidia Gonzalez Seco, Robin Clement, Kristen Cañizares, and Peter Rosset.

Bachman, Hewart. 2005. "The Other Progress Days." *Rural Heritage* 30 (6): 59.

Berry, Wendell. 2005. "Renewing husbandry." *Orion* Online. Accessed 29 June 2006, http://www.oriononline.org/pages/om/05-5om/Berry.html.

Bialik, Carl. 2006. "Digging into the Ethanol Debate." *Wall Street Journal* On-line, 6 June 2006. Accessed 10 June 2006: http://online.wsj.com/public/article/SB114970102238673892-mFUS5_VqqxV6nw3agvv9M4kmiX4_20060708.html?mod=tff_main_tff_top.

Conroy, Drew. 2005. "Cuba's Organic Production." *Rural Heritage* 30 (6): 72–75.

Conroy, Drew. 2001. "Mechanization, animal traction, and sustainable agriculture." pp. 155–163 in Fernando Funes, et al., eds. *Sustainable Agriculture and Resistance*. Oakland, CA: Food First Books, 2001.

de Madriaga, Salvador. 1947. *The Rise of the Spanish American Empire*. New York: The Free Press/Macmillen, 1947.

Diamond, Jared. 2004. *Collapse: How Societies Choose to Fail or Succeed*. New York: Penguin.

Encyclopedia Brittanica, 1968. "Farm Machinery." Vol. 9, p. 88.

Graham, Wade. 2005. "The Jolly Green Giant." *On Earth* 27 (Fall): 14–19.

Guinness Book of World Records. New York: Bantam Books, 1988. 26th ed.

Jackson, Wes. 2002. "Natural Systems Agriculture: A radical alternative." *Agriculture, Ecosystems and Environment* 88: 111–117.

Johnson, Walter A. Victor Stoltzfus, and Peter Craumer. 1977. "Energy Conservation in Amish Agriculture." *Science* 198: 373–378.

Langdon, John. 1986. *Horses, Oxen and Technological Innovation: The Use of Draught Animals in English Farming from 1066 to 1500*. London: Cambridge University Press.

Morrison, F.B. 1941. *Feeds and Feeding*. Ithaca, NY: The Morrison Publishing Co. 20th ed.

Mumford, Lewis. 1933. *Technics and Civilization*. London and New York: Harcourt, Brace, and Jovanovich.

Pimentel, David, and Tad W. Patzek. 2005. "Ethanol Production Using Corn, Switchgrass, and Wood; Biodiesel Production Using Soybean and Sunflower." *Natural Resources Research* 14(1): 65–76.

Ramaswamy, N. 1994. "Draught Animals and Welfare." *Review of Science and Technology* O. I. E. 13: 195–216.

Schnepf, Randy. 2004. *Energy Use in Agriculture.* Library of Congress, Congressional Research Service Report for Congress, Order Code RL32677. 11/19/2004.

Stinner, Deborah H., M. G. Paoletti, and B. R. Stinner. 1989. "In Search of Traditional Farm Wisdom for a More Sustainable Agriculture: A Study of Amish Farming and Society." *Agriculture, Ecosystems, and Environment* 27: 77–90.

Telleen, Maurice. 1977. *The Draft Horse Primer.* Emmaus, PA: Rodale Press.

Thomas, Dylan. 1971. *The Poems of Dylan Thomas.* NY: New Directions Publishing Corp.

Warren, G. F. 1910. *The Elements of Agriculture.* New York: Macmillan.

Traveler, There is No Road
(Caminante, No Hay Camino)

My translation of a poem by Antonio Machado

Caminante, No Hay Camino
Caminante, son tus huellas
el camino y nada más;
Caminante, no hay camino,
se hace camino al andar.
Al andar se hace el camino,
y al volver la vista atrás
se ve la senda que nunca
se ha de volver a pisar.
Caminante, no hay camino
sino estelas en la mar.

Traveler, there is No Road
Traveler, there is no road
but the road you leave behind,
Traveler, the road you make,
is the only road you'll find.
You make the path as you walk along
and as you backward gaze,
You see the tracks that nevermore,
your footsteps may retrace.
Traveler, there is no road,
just a wake upon the waves.

Dick's Maxims

Beware adventitious opportunity.

There are no small jobs. Only small jobs that turn into big jobs.

Never violate your own rules. Others' rules, maybe. Never your own.

Small sums of money should not exchange hands between friends.

Never lend to a friend any more than you're willing to write off as a gift, without harm to the friendship.

Put it in its place (so you can find it). Habit is much stronger than memory.

Do it today. It won't be any easier tomorrow.

Acknowledgments

This would be a lesser book without the drawings of my brilliant long-time illustrator and collaborator, Maeve Courteau. Award-winning photographers including our son Caleb Courteau, Beverly Conley, Don House, and my son Dan Kasztelan contributed from their fine photos. My son-in-law Paul Graham proofread the manuscript meticulously. No book at all would have made it into print without the tireless efforts of my daughter, Dr. Jacqueline Belle Courteau. "Jackie," as I have called her since a baby, has assumed the task of "project manager" for my writing. She types every manuscript from my crude hand-writing, communicates with my editors, and performs all administrative work.

I am grateful to Joe Mischka, and to his partner Susan Blocker, for taking interest in my writings and publishing them over the past several years in their fine magazine, *Rural Heritage.* It is from those published articles that much of the material in this book is drawn. I am grateful to Joe for the fine layout and design work that he does for my articles in the pages of the magazine, and for generously taking on the layout and design of this book.

Also, thanks to the folks at Mission Point Press, including editors/project managers Mark Lewison and Misha Neidorfler, proofreader Hart Cauchy, Janella Williams for the cover design, and Tricia Frey for bookstore outreach and publicity. Thanks to Walsworth for the beautiful print edition of this book, which was produced on Sterling Premium Crown Gloss with 10% recycled fiber content.

I feel that I should acknowledge posthumously a few major providers of aid in helping me develop the skills and knowledge behind the writing of this book. First and foremost, Joanna Wojtowicz Courteau, my Polish-born first wife, whose moral and material support enabled me to return to farm and ranch life, where I was to continue to hone my equine knowledge. Two other Poles, the American-born Vic and Eddie Sobieleski, provided me, during their wintry Minnesota sleigh-ride business, my first instruction in horsemanship of any kind. Joe Lowther, a mixed-blood Crow Indian in Montana, taught me the graceful seat on horseback that I was to maintain into my eighties. Down in Wyoming, Leonard LaDue (I've never known the exact spelling), another mixed Crow and a veteran of World War II, taught me the tricks of getting a "bronc" started in harness.

In recognition of the importance of the printed word in passing down the ancient craft of horsemanship, I point out—among the very long list of those who have furnished me with principles and techniques—four of the writers who have most influenced me:

- Harry Chamberlin, in his *Training Hunters, Jumpers, and Hacks,* laid a firm, thorough foundation in the basic principles;
- Charles O. Williamson, in his *Breaking and Training the Stock Horse,* applies those principles to the training of the cow horse (or just generally Western-style horsemanship);
- Ed Connell, in *Hackamore Reinsman,* teaches the California (Mexico, Spain) method of starting a colt without a bit); and
- Monte Foreman's *Horse Handling Science* is instructive in all—I studied, with particular interest, his handling of the fast stop.

Even though it's not down in "the ol' barnyard," the printed page often carries distilled wisdom. Read, young horse-folks!

About the Author and Illustrators

Author **Dick Courteau's** earliest memories, from infancy, are of seeing horses at work. He has been riding and working horses—and then donkeys and some mules—since age eleven, when his foster father gave him his first pony, the stone-blind but spirited twelve-hand pinto mare Toots. He has lived an itinerant life centered around working with horses, and more recently, donkeys. His book on donkey training, *Get Your Ass to Work! An Illustrated Guide to Training Your Donkey to Harness* (Mission Point Press 2020), has been called "indispensable reading." He started contributing essays and how-to tips to *Rural Heritage* magazine in 2020, and has been a regular contributor since 2021.

PHOTO: CALEB COURTEAU

PHOTO: CALEB COURTEAU

Illustrator *Maeve Courteau*, once artist-in-residence for Terra Studios in Durham, Arkansas, is best known for her widely marketed art-carved wooden spoons, but is a master at interpreting animals, whether in sculpture, in paint, or on the sketchpad. Her drawings were an essential part of *Get Your Ass to Work!* and have illustrated many of Dick's articles in *Rural Heritage.*

Guest author and project manager *Jacqueline Courteau* is a biologist and writer who has ridden and written with father Dick since she was a child. She has contributed several pieces to *Rural Heritage*, and she has typed manuscripts, compiled photos, and coordinated layout and publication for his articles and books.

PHOTOGRAPHERS

Beverly Conley is a documentary photographer whose rural series includes the photo essay, "Life in the Ozarks: An Arkansas Portrait" (https://www.beverlyconleyphotography.com). She has exhibited widely in major museums and is represented in the permanent collections of The Smithsonian and The Museum of London.

Caleb Courteau is a photographer who has worked as an industrial mechanic and is currently training in technical education. He has exhibited his photos in local galleries in Northwest Arkansas, and was the photographer for *Get Your Ass to Work!* as well as contributing to various of Dick's *Rural Heritage* articles. He likes to photograph nature and find unique angles.

Don House has been photographing and writing about the people and landscapes of the Arkansas Ozarks for nearly four decades (https://www.donhousephotoworks.com). His images and words have appeared in numerous exhibitions and publications as diverse as *The Wall Street Journal* and *Boy's Life.* He is the author of four books, including: *Letters to Dan: A Philosophical Guide to the Ozarks*, and *Remote Access: Small Public Libraries in Arkansas.* When he is not wandering the woods, or floating the rivers, he lives and works and ponders in Hazel Valley, in rural Washington County.

Daniel J. Kasztelan is director of communications for a Quaker non-profit organization, Friends United Meeting. He is editor and chief photographer for *Quaker Life,* where his photographs can be regularly found. He lives with his wife Suzanne in rural Indiana, where they raise sheep for wool.

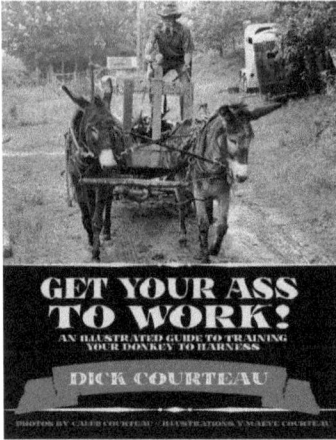

"There are few books in the world that provide such a comprehensive wealth of useful and detailed information on a topic they may be labeled indispensable reading. Dick Courteau has put together just such a book [on] donkeys."

— Joe Mischka, Editor & Publisher, *Rural Heritage*

"...finally the donkeys have their own book.... I hope this book inspires a new generation of donkeys and people working together..."

— Charlie Tennessen, *Rural Heritage* contributor

"...this book is also a visual delight... [with] a healthy dose of hard-won humor..."

— Stephen Leslie, author of *Horse-Powered Farming for the 21st Century (2015)*

"...a book from someone who's given more thought to donkeys and their training than most people give to anything at all..."

— *Arkansas Life* magazine

Dick Courteau's earlier work, *Get Your Ass to Work!*, offers a comprehensive guide for training donkeys to harness for use on small farms and homesteads. The book appeals even to those who don't own donkeys, resonating with rural residents and animal enthusiasts alike. The book contains beautiful illustrations and poignant reflections on the role of working animals and country living, and offers a delightful exploration of the relationship between humans and their four-legged companions.

Available only on our website or through *Rural Heritage* magazine. To order the book and check out some of Dick's other writings, visit his website: getyourasstowork.com.

www.ingramcontent.com/pod-product-compliance
Lightning Source LLC
Chambersburg PA
CBHW052016030426
42335CB00026B/3165